If You Could See the World Through My Eyes...

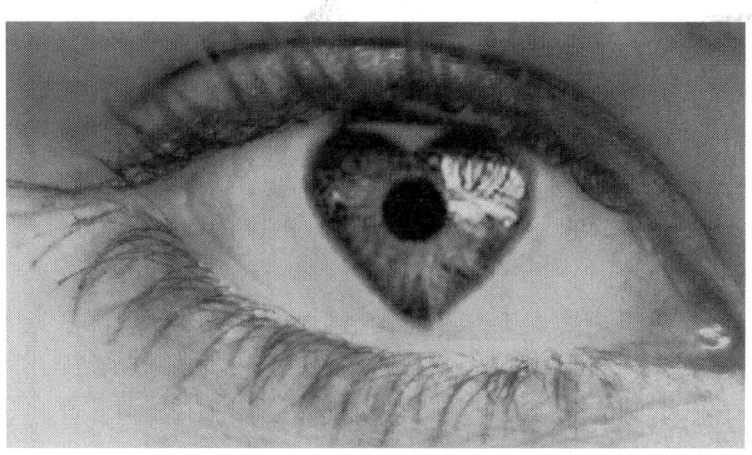

Some Lessons on Life from a Psychic Medium

Andrea Claire

Sending you lots of love!
Andrea Claire ♡

Table of Contents

DEDICATION..1
MORE THANKS...3
FINDING THE HAPPY MEDIUM........................6
AWARENESS & ACCEPTANCE.......................12
BE TRUE TO YOURSELF.................................20
PLAYING THE NAME GAME..........................28
MY LIFETIME OF ADVENTURE.....................39
BE GRATEFUL..45
BE OPEN-MINDED...57
BE DISCERNING..71
BE PRESENT..81
BE POSITIVE..91
BE ACCEPTING..99
BE WILLING TO BREAK A SWEAT...............117
BE KIND..135
BE FORGIVING..143
ALOHA!...153

DEDICATION

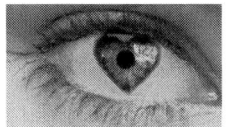

To anyone who knows me, it should come as no surprise that this book is dedicated to my son, Drew.

There is never a day that goes by that I don't thank God for having Drew in my life. He is the biggest part of my heart, and I love him "all the way to the moon and back"!

I was spiritually awakened when Drew was born. Throughout the entire pregnancy, I was well aware that there was a Higher Power working with us both, overseeing and ensuring his safe delivery into the world.

Drew has played a huge role in teaching me about

unconditional love, patience, tolerance, and compassion. He keeps me present and appreciative of every moment.

Being a Mom forced me to become more responsible. Drew's unwavering faith in me pushes me to higher levels. He has patiently stood by me, and always encourages me to continue on this path, especially when the going gets tough.

Thank you, Drew, for being my voice of reason, for keeping me grounded, and for making me stay true to myself and to you.

Thank you for choosing me and challenging me to be the Mother that you deserve to have. Thank you for inspiring me to write this book.

All that I am and all that I am meant to become is because of, and dedicated to you …

MORE THANKS

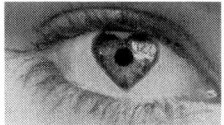

I wish to express my heartfelt appreciation to a few important others who play key roles in my life.

First and foremost, thank you God for continuing to use me as Your conduit of love and enlightenment. You are my "CSO" (Chief Spiritual Officer), and it's in Your hands that I place my faith and trust. I know that You're the one running this show, and I am your willing assistant.

Thank you to my Guides who patiently teach me and challenge me to grow. My Guides are my team of Wise beings on The Other Side who are helping me in this lifetime. They encourage, they "correct", they educate, and they have sometimes had to intervene on my behalf. They help me continue to honour my spiritual contracts in this lifetime.

Thank you to everyone who has supported me in my work, including my students, clients, and friends. Thank you for confiding in me, and for sharing your stories with me. You will always be my inspiration to work harder and become even more clear as a conduit of love and light.

Thanks to my friend Leo Vincent for acknowledging me as having been your Spiritual Teacher in your book <u>Angels Calling: Miracles of a Telephone Repairman</u>. I am touched that I have supported you in your personal journey.

I am much obliged to world-renowned Psychic Medium John Edward. He is my role model! John Edward has blazed the trail and raised the bar in educating the masses. He made it so much easier for me to step out in this capacity as a Psychic Medium. He keeps it REAL and remains humble. I appreciate his honesty, his integrity, his "pit bull" demeanour, and his stellar display of Psychic Mediumship.

Finally, a long distance prayer of thanks goes outward (and upward) to my dear friend, Ryan Unger. Our time together as friends wasn't long enough, however I am ever so grateful that our paths did cross. You taught me so much in such a short period of time.

I promised Ryan that he would be the first person to receive an autographed copy of my book. Sadly, the timing was off. Rest in peace, my friend. You were always a busy man when I knew you, and I expect that you continue to be the same in Spirit. Hopefully you can find some time to read this on the Other Side.

Cheers!

FINDING THE HAPPY MEDIUM

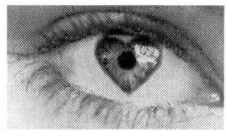

My name is Andrea Claire, and I am a Psychic Medium. I acknowledge I am somewhat different from others, however I don't feel that I am special. Being a Psychic Medium might make me unique, but I'm not inclined to see myself as being extraordinary. I'm just me.

We all play many roles in life, and are defined by the responsibilities of each. In addition to serving as Psychic Medium, I am also a mother, sister, friend, Business Owner, Counselor, Motivational Speaker, and a human being (wink!).

I doubt that they would ever produce a television show based on my life as a Psychic Medium. The movies and reality shows tend to dramatize what goes on in a day in the life of a Psychic Medium!

When I am "off duty" (not working as a Psychic Medium), I lead a fairly ordinary life. I drive to my appointments. I cook, I clean (sometimes!), and I do laundry. I make grocery lists and forget to bring them with me. The older I get, the more I seem to be forgetting! I laugh. I cry. I sing (poorly). I hang out with my friends. I like to huddle under a blanket watching chick flicks and romance movies. I abhor violence of any kind. I take naps. I get frustrated. I can be impatient. I have good hair days, and I have bad hair days. I make mistakes, I apologize, and I strive to do better the next time.

I go out every day looking pretty average. I do not sensationalize or make an effort to stand out. I keep things real, and for the most part, I blend in with the mainstream. You'd never pick me out of the crowd as a Psychic Medium unless you already knew me in this capacity.

I remain under the spotlight as much as possible, so I can keep my personal life private. I cherish the moments I have to myself and use them to relax, regroup, and spend time with my loved ones. Friends and family are very important to me.

I have always been fascinated with human behaviour and the desire to figure out what makes people "tick". I graduated from Brock University in 1983 with a Bachelor of Arts degree in Sociology, and minored in Psychology. While my original goal was to become a Counselor upon graduating, it didn't turn out that way. A few other things had to fall into place first.

I believe that one cannot effectively counsel others in crisis without having some relateable experience. I endured a lot of major life lessons before I felt prepared to step forward to assist and enlighten others. Recollecting how I had felt when facing and overcoming similar difficulties, I am very empathetic. Clients feel my genuine compassion and sincerity. I deeply care about their welfare, however I have to distance myself emotionally from their outcomes. It would otherwise become too overwhelming for me.

After graduating from University, I held several different jobs, including Receptionist, Administrative Assistant, Accounts Receivable Clerk, Information Counselor, and Computer Systems Administrator. I also owned an Interior Decorating business.

It appears to be a multifaceted career path but, in hindsight, each job I held served to better prepare me for my current role as a Psychic Medium. I learned the fine art of communication, of listening, of relating to their situation, of supporting others, and was always challenged to expand my knowledge. Moreover, I gained the skills required to manage and market my own business.

I was born, raised, and continue to live in the City of St. Catharines, Ontario (Canada). I had high hopes of moving somewhere more "exciting", but it never panned out. Instead, I did what was fairly typical for most people my age. I found a full-time job, I paid off my student loans, I met a really nice guy, we dated, we got engaged, we bought a home, we got married, and seven years later we welcomed a beautiful son into our world. Despite the trials and tribulations, I built a decent life for myself.

In retrospect, I am so happy that I didn't move away from St. Catharines after all. Life is less chaotic in a smaller city. Our "rush hour" lasts approximately twenty minutes. All amenities are within reach.

The city is perfectly situated in the heart of the Niagara Region. We have dozens of local wineries producing award-winning wines. So too, it lies within the Niagara Fruit belt, where the majority of Ontario's tender fruit crops are grown.

The Welland Canal is one of the amazing man-made wonders of the world, and its first three locks are in St. Catharines. Although we locals complain whenever the bridge is raised, the Welland Canal is truly a marvel to behold.

I live quite close to the beach, and can watch the

most breathtaking sunsets on Lake Ontario.

A variety of tourist destinations are a stone's throw away, namely Niagara Falls and the historic town of Niagara-on-the-Lake. I'm only a two hour drive from Toronto, and a thirty minute drive to the United States border. There are three major airports in close proximity. It's so easy to plan an escape without stressing over the logistics!

Home is where the heart is, and my heart will always remain in Niagara.

My life is so simple, and yet so grand. I am abundantly blessed on many levels.

I sincerely am "The Happy Medium"!

AWARENESS & ACCEPTANCE

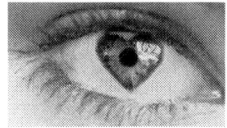

I am often asked when I became aware that I was a Psychic Medium. For the record, I have always been a Psychic and a Medium, but I avoided accepting those labels. I neither realized, appreciated, nor acted in this capacity until much later in my life.

To be totally honest, I was living in denial.

As a child, I experienced many psychic events, including déjá-vu's, prophetic dreams, and seeing ghosts. Although seeing ghosts really spooked me (pun *intended!*), I didn't think to question what was happening. This was my "normal", and I assumed that everyone was this way. Better yet, I think I wanted to believe that everyone was just like me, for fear of discovering that I might actually be "different".

For as long as I can remember, I have been trusted as the voice of reason. People would ask for my advice, and I would be "blurting" answers and predictions that clearly weren't emanating from me. Divine guidance flowed seamlessly through me. I connected with people without even realizing that I was connecting. Again, I neither appreciated nor understood the gifts that were working with me and through me at the time.

I used to go for readings, and the Psychics would inform me that *I* should be the one giving **them** a reading! That didn't make sense to me at all.

In my forties, I became more aware of the intensity of my psychic abilities. I toyed with the idea that I **might** have some extraordinary skills, but I remained skeptical. I wanted more proof. I didn't want to stand out. I was very reluctant to admit the truth, not only to myself, but also to friends, business associates, and family members. "Fitting in" was really important to me. To a certain degree, it still is.

My safe and predictable life permanently changed in the year 2001. To this day, I still don't know whether I was going through a mid-life crisis, or if my spiritual "alarm clock" was blaring. I definitely woke up that year and made some changes.

The pressures in my career were climbing, and I quit my full-time job. My marriage was rocky, and my ex and I separated. It seems that I had walked away from everyone and everything that had previously defined me – with the exception of my son. I would never abandon him. Ours is a sacred life contract.

Everyone else thought I had lost my mind! I began wondering the same. It took a bit of time for me to process everything that had happened, get my head in order, and figure out my next plan.

I look back at this now and know that my world was shaken up to force me to step on my spiritual path. Being prone to child-like behaviour, I stubbornly fought against it.

In 2002, I received certification in Interior Design. Then I attended an Entrepreneurship training program. With that education to support me, I opened an Interior Decorating business.

I noticed that my clients weren't commenting about the tangible changes in their home, but instead mentioned how "wonderful they felt" in their newly decorated spaces. Curiosity got the better of me, and I studied Colour Therapy. I learned about the energy and vibration of colours, and used that in conjunction with my own intuition to "read" the needs of my clients. I purposely chose colour palettes that would complement their lives. My business motto became "Making Your Home Your Sanctuary".

I thought that this was a clever way to utilize my psychic gifts, without having to confess what was truly going on backstage. I could remain cloaked behind the more socially acceptable title of Interior Decorator.

I was only fooling myself, though. There were other Divine designs unfolding on my behalf. Those plans were bigger than I could even begin to imagine and accept.

My life exploded for the second time in the year 2007, primarily as an opportunity to literally be cemented to my path. My bullheadedness was dramatically going to be tested.

Competition was fierce and my interior decorating business collapsed. I was applying for all sorts of jobs, but wasn't getting hired. My divorce was finalized, and I had obstinately waived all means of support in that agreement. I was a single parent with a young child to raise, a condo to maintain, bills to pay, and food to put on the table. I was scared.

In addition, my parents were very sick that year. I spent a lot of time visiting each of them in hospitals and nursing homes. Mom died in October. Dad died a few months after her. It was a grueling time.

My resistance and reluctance to embrace my path kind of became like a game of "musical chairs". I kept grabbing at any chair available whenever the music stopped, until there were no chairs left...

Being painted into a corner at that point, I dropped to my knees and had a conversation with God.

Why was all of this happening all at once? Where should I turn now? What was it that I was meant to do? Why can't I find a job? How could I afford to live? Is there some other way that I could be of service?? I took that scary trip inward, meditated, prayed and searched my heart of hearts for an answer.

I discovered a pattern developing. Every time that I would ask God and my Guides for direction, I would receive a few emails or phone calls from friends afterwards. They were either asking me for my advice, or thanking me because the advice I had given them really worked out!

I started connecting the dots.

It was clearer to me that it was time to make things official. I was meant to be of service in the capacity of Psychic Medium.

Although I trust the advice from my Guides implicitly, stepping out in my true identity required taking a huge leap of faith. I took a big breath, and surrendered.

It didn't take long before I was shown new opportunities to be self-supporting. I rose to the challenges. I attended a networking event and offered complimentary five minute readings. There was a lineup out the door! People started booking appointments. Then they told others about me, and their friends and family booked appointments too. Word was spreading, and I was awestruck. The City of St. Catharines agreed to host a series of seminars I had developed to educate others about "all things spiritual". I am still teaching with them to this day.

My Guides paved the path and made the transition much easier than I ever expected it would be.

Looking back now, I understand and appreciate that my Guides were not imposing **their** will on me. Instead, they were reminding me about the soul contract that I had agreed to honour in this lifetime.

My full-time practice as a Psychic Medium has afforded me the distinct honour of meeting so many intriguing people. It has gifted me with some alternative and unique perspectives on life and living. It has granted me "access" to Divine insights and information from the Wise and Loving souls on the Other Side.

I am so thankful that I finally accepted my calling as Psychic Medium. I don't know why I chose to fight it so adamantly. I remain in a state of awe and humility that I am trusted to serve in this capacity.

It has been an incredible adventure thus far.

BE TRUE TO YOURSELF

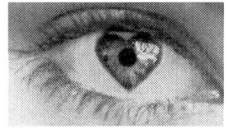

"There is no greater agony than
bearing an untold story inside you."
(Maya Angelou)

I still regard my most important role in life as being a supportive and loving Mom to my son. He is my world, and I pray that I have taught him a lot by being who I am and doing what I do. I am very proud of the young man he has become, and am thrilled to be known as his Mom. Sure, we butt heads once in awhile. We disagree about some things, but we agree about most things. The pulse of our relationship will always be love and respect.

The rest of the world perceives and labels me as a Psychic Medium. It's the identity that raises the most eyebrows, and I have learned to deal with it. I'm not going for the "shock factor" when I tell people that I'm a Medium, but it tends to be their reaction.

In order to do what I do for a living, you have to develop true strength, resilience, clear boundaries, and a healthy sense of humour. I am definitely quite a character!

After more than a decade of establishing my full-time practice, I am becoming known as Niagara's Psychic Medium. While I work diligently in the Niagara area, my client base continues to expand throughout Canada and the United States.

Mediumship can be performed as effectively by phone and Skype, thus I have also served clients who live as far away as Ireland, the Caribbean, and Barcelona. I am awestruck and ever so grateful for the opportunities that keep coming! Technology has made the boundaries of communication seamless. Because of this, my practice continues to grow and that I am able to serve a wider audience.

I have been judged and dismissed for the work I do (even by people I love), and I will admit that it hurts.

This never stops me from being who I am, believing what I know as truth, and doing what I do.

On the contrary, I have also been dearly respected and loved for the work that I do. That helps to soften the blows.

Being a bit of an enigma, people will make wrongful assumptions about who I am and the gifts with which I have been blessed. That's okay, I understand! It is human nature to attack and criticize things that people don't understand. C'est la vie!

If I lived my life by constantly justifying who I am, all that I represent, and the work that I do, then I wouldn't be authentically Andrea Claire!

I am actively in the public eye demonstrating the practice of Psychic Mediumship. I am speaking to larger crowds now, yet strive to keep it intimate. I never take anything for granted and remain appreciative of every opportunity I am afforded.

Some do not understand why I am the way I am, and won't dig deeper to find the answers. If you ask me anything about myself, I will always give you a genuine answer! My life is an open book. I have nothing to hide. It's so much easier to live in truth.

I abide by self-prescribed ethical principles. I have aligned with people whose behaviours did not resonate with mine, and I've had to walk away from them. At the end of the day, I have to adhere to my moral code.

Some people have told me that I should "lighten up", which is ironic when you think about it. I do like to go out and have fun, but I'm not your typical party commando. I learned in a marketing class that each and every time you step outside of your home, you are a walking, talking billboard of who you are and what you represent.

I took that to heart.

When I'm not working, I am NOT open to receiving messages from the Spirit world. You might be surprised to learn that I can willingly turn the element of Mediumship "on" and "off".

In order to connect to the Other Side, I raise my vibration as high as I can to match that of Spirit (they are always with us, but vibrate much faster than we humans do). Holding that connection can be physically taxing, and requires that I follow a certain protocol in order to raise and keep my vibration that high. That being said, I only do so when I am acting in the capacity as a Psychic Medium.

I would never walk through a mall "fully open", because I could conceivably self-destruct in about five seconds!

A friend of mine told me that sometimes she is afraid to chat with me, because she thinks I am "reading" into her when we are together. I assured her that I wasn't. I am merely interested and want to catch up!

I sincerely care about people, but I don't offer advice unless asked to do so.

I feel that it's a huge ethical breach to go around reading other people without their permission. I am not the one who will tap you on the shoulder in the food court and tell you that your dead Mom is sitting beside you watching you eat that burger and fries. That's just not my style!

When they find out that I am a Psychic Medium, sometimes people will ask if I can give them a quick reading on the spot. I smile and tell them that I could, but I won't. I don't appreciate being used like that.

If you bumped into your chiropractor in the grocery store, would you ask him for a quick adjustment right there in the frozen food section? I highly doubt it. Even if you did, I am confidant that he would recommend that you call his office and book an appointment instead.

I am NOT a mind-reader, either. People will ask me "Can you tell me what I'm thinking right now?", and I shake my head. No I can't, nor would I ever want to.

Other Psychic Mediums may conduct themselves differently. It's not my place to judge. These are MY rules and MY boundaries that I have imposed in the name of self-protection and self-preservation. My rules keep me grounded and extremely real.

Every day is a whole new day, and there is always something fresh to learn. I continue to train and grow, to adapt and refine, and to hone and share these gifts, in the name of service, for others.

I am firmly rooted in knowing that the soul is eternal, there is a very active and vibrant life after life, and the bonds of love are never-ending.

I won't force my truths down your throat. It is not my intention to convert the naysayers and make everyone a "believer" of the Spirit World.

This is not a popularity contest for me. Either you believe or you don't. It's your choice to make.

Maybe I'll get you thinking, though. I enjoy doing that. Get to know me better, and I'll really challenge you to expand your awareness. I genuinely love an inquiring mind. There is SO MUCH more to this life than meets the eye.

Your life is your story that you scripted before birth. You chose the key actors and events to encourage your growth.

Be true to yourself and be true to the story that you are writing. Sing your song, dance your dance, and don't ever hold back on living your life in full colour!

"To be yourself in a world that is constantly trying to make you something else is the greatest accomplishment."
(Ralph Waldo Emerson)

PLAYING THE NAME GAME

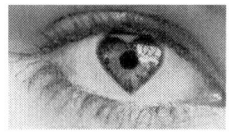

"Proper names are rigid designators."
(Saul Kripke)

Your name is your unique identifier and interestingly enough, it carries with it a certain vibration and meaning. When I "connect" with clients, I connect firstly with their name. Their name is the energetic key that unlocks the door and permits me access to what lies beneath and within them. Interestingly enough, Spirit will "choose" the name that they will connect with. I have often discovered that they prefer to connect with one's proper name, and not with a nickname or abbreviated version.

Once I was trying to connect with a client who stated his name as "Billy". I couldn't connect with that name to save my life. I then asked him to state his **proper** name. When he said, "William", the connection was made.

It's interesting how we can energetically alter our identity when we abbreviate our given name.

I went through a period of "Who am I?" when my divorce was finalized. I grieved the fact that a huge chunk of my life was now "dead". For fourteen years, I had been defined by my marriage, and had built an identity and life with that name. My ex and I were so aligned to the rest of the world, that our names had kind of morphed into ONE name!

That chapter of my life was officially closed. I grieved its ending like one would mourn someone's passing. Eventually I had to accept the reality.

As Psychic Medium John Edward says, "When you take the 'u' out of 'mourning', it's a whole new day!"

If you constantly dwell on the past, and obsess about the disappointments, you miss out on seeing the great possibilities that lie directly ahead of you!

It was time to start embracing my future.

Knowing that changing my name meant that I would also be altering the meaning and vibration of my identity, I gave this careful consideration. I felt greatly detached from my married name. It no longer fit.

I chose to drop my last name, thereby permitting my son to live his life without a tie by name to me. This would absolve him of being judged because of what his Mom did for a living. (Ironically my son is one of my greatest marketers and supporters, and proudly identifies with me.)

I have always been and will always be Andrea Claire. Those are my actual first and middle names! To this day, I still thank my parents for naming me Andrea Claire!

I'm often asked if my name is a stage name. Obviously it isn't. I'm not an actress assuming a role.

This is who I truly am!

Using the names Andrea Claire solely (and soully) would completely free me on an energetic level, and allow me to independently and clearly step into my true capacity.

One day I was chatting with a friend who is also a Psychic (it's always nice to have a Psychic in your back pocket!). She asked, "Have you ever anagrammed your name to see the hidden meaning behind it?"

Anagrams are plays on words, where you rearrange the letters in a word to form new words or phrases. It's a fun way to decode and decipher hidden meanings!

Always looking for a new bone to chew on, I found an anagram generator on the internet, and typed in Andrea Claire.

The anagram generator chugged away and finally the box popped up: "REAL RADIANCE".

Seriously?

That surprised me. I want to emphasize that there is NO ego attached to my work. I don't put myself on a pedestal. But that anagram was pretty cool!

The expression "real radiance" embodies my ultimate goal in being of service: In embracing the ethical and moral responsibilities of Psychic Mediumship, I strive to be the brightest conduit of love and light that I can be. My prayer is always to connect with the highest and the best in Spirit, and deliver clear, accurate, and timely messages for my clients' greatest good.

An interesting association with the name is that, as a Psychic Medium, my gifts include **Claircognizance, Clairsentience, Clairaudience, Clairvoyance, Clairalience, and Clairempathy.**

Here is a brief description of each gift:

Claircognizance refers to clear knowing. When I connect with a client, Spirit will start feeding me very personal and private details about them (which often freaks them out!) without my having prior knowledge of the information. This also includes knowing details of their past, present, and future without any physical explanation or reason.

Clairsentience refers to clear sensing of emotions and physical ailments. Most people recall how their loved one died. Spirit will use that as validation that it truly is them coming through! For example, Spirit will build on me the sensation of a heart attack or cancer. One time my right leg went completely numb from the knee down, and, as it turned out, the Mom in spirit was an amputee and used that as her "calling card" to identify her presence.

Clairaudience refers to clear hearing of voices, sounds, and thoughts from Spirit. I can distinguish between the voices from Spirit and those of the everyday world, because theirs will come through just underneath my right ear. Their voices are always quiet, calm and detached.

Clairvoyance refers to clearly seeing visions, images, and pictures. I don't witness these images in the same manner that I see things through my human eyes. On the contrary, I view them through my "mind's eye" (or third eye). The best way I can describe it is that I am shown pictures, images, or "scenes" at the end of a long tunnel. I have to remain focused on what I am being shown, rather than on the client's reaction to what is being said.

Clairailience refers to clear smelling. Sometimes Spirit will use their "signature scent" like perfume or after-shave (Old Spice is a frequent one!), the smell of cigarette or pipe smoke (if the deceased was a smoker), or the smell of alcohol (if the deceased had alcohol issues) as an identifier.

Clairempathy refers to clearly experiencing what others are feeling. This is definitely the most taxing of my gifts . When I connect with clients, it's almost as if I am "inside" them, feeling what they are feeling, remembering their memories, and living their life. I am able to sense their attitudes, emotions, and ailments.

Communicating with Spirit requires that those in Spirit have various ways and means in order to relay their messages. When I "tap" into my clients, a whole bunch of senses kick into play to assist in the reading.

To put it in layman terms, I present to those in Spirit my toy box of "clair" gifts which they can use to communicate through me. It's up to them – and to my Guides – to determine which one(s) are utilized.

There are some in Spirit who are really awesome at getting their messages across, and some who aren't. It's part of THEIR learning curve over there! Some rely on symbols and signs, while others can speak directly (telepathically) to me.

There is an enormous amount of work going on behind the scenes in order to deliver messages from Spirit. There are a series of "permissions" that must be met – it's comparable to the "read/write/execute" of software programming. If conditions are met, then messages are delivered.

Our Guides and Loved Ones in Spirit are always eager to assist you with their guidance, yet there are always exceptions to this rule.

For example, if the person I am reading is in the middle of a major life lesson, their Guides and Loved Ones are silent. It is not their intention or responsibility to give information that will solve this lesson on behalf of my client. This can be frustrating and I certainly commiserate with my clients when this happens. However, it is out of absolute love and faith that they know better than to interfere with your important life lessons. They will continue to watch over you and quietly lend their support.

Another situation I experienced in my work really opened my eyes. I met with a client who had just had a reading with another Psychic, and was devastated by what she had been told. Apparently, absolutely every decision she had made to date had been incorrect, according to that Psychic.

When I connected with her, the messages that came through were fast, furious, and extremely positive. Several times in the reading, we BOTH broke out in goosebumps (which is a sign of validation).

I am not one to deliver "feel good" messages simply to spare my client. There is a huge burden of responsibility to this work, knowing that you have the capability of directly impacting those you read.

I questioned her Guides and asked why the information they were giving was so different from her previous reading.

Their response startled me. They said, "We would never choose to work with that other reader." In other words, that other Psychic wasn't even connected to the client's Guides when reading her.

I consulted with a friend of mine in this field of work, and asked her if she had ever heard of something like that before. She told me that she had not, but felt that it made perfect sense when you stop to think about it.

These examples are only a few of the numerous rules governing Mediumship. There are so many other things going on behind the scenes that result in the delivery of a message. I won't get into the mechanics of Mediumship in this book.

If you are curious, there are a lot of websites that discuss what is going on "backstage" with the practice of Mediumship. Seek them out for yourself!

MY LIFETIME OF ADVENTURE

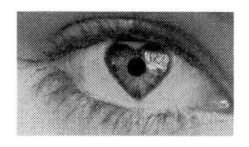

I have, either deliberately or accidentally thrown myself into an unbelievable number of lessons in this lifetime. My life has not always been easy. Most people mistakenly think that I live a charmed life. Let me assure you that I don't.

I am not one to whimper incessantly about things. Sure, I'll sound off for a bit, but then I will make a valiant effort to figure things out. After all, complaining without seeking resolution is called whining. I don't like to whine. Sometimes I succeed through trial and error. For the most part, I have learned to lean upon my intuition, and to get quiet and listen to what that small voice inside me suggests.

I view my life as a work in progress. I see meaning

and purpose in every experience I have encountered. Every person who has crossed my path has served a purpose in pushing me forward and helping me learn some tough lessons. My life, like yours, is a direct reflection of those choices I have made, and those I have refused we to make.

We have all been blessed with the gift of free will. We are entitled to choose whatever we want or do not want to experience.

Accepting this truth requires that one takes ownership of their life. No longer will you be permitted to point the finger of blame in the opposite direction. One of my often-used expressions is "if you enable it, you deserve it". And yes, that phrase has slapped me a few times too.

I am frequently asked if I can read myself. My answer is always, "I WISH!!". Clearly I can't even predict the winning lottery numbers for myself (wink!).

This is one of the biggest misconceptions about being a Psychic Medium. People assume that I know it all. I will be the first to admit that I don't! Seriously, if you ever meet someone who declares that they DO know it all, run as fast as you can in the opposite direction. Life is a continuous journey of discovery. It is not our purpose to know everything there is to learn.

The information and advice that I channel comes from a Source much wiser than me, and I am honoured to be able to relay this Divine wisdom to those whom I counsel. I learn and attempt to retain so much information in the process.

My gifts are gifts of service – to others – and not to myself. It is my understanding that any breach in this rule results in the immediate revocation of said gifts. In other words, if these gifts are used to scam or hurt or manipulate or trespass against others, Spirit will deactivate them. I have personally witnessed this happen to others who were once quite gifted readers.

I am perfectly imperfect. I confess that I have stumbled and fumbled at times in my life! I have experienced some EPIC fails! Conversely, I have also enjoyed some awesome successes!

I have loved intensely, and have had my heart broken (too many times to count). Just when I think I've seen or heard it all, I am surprised (and/or shocked!!) by something new. I have unintentionally hurt people, and I am truly sorry for having done so. People have hurt me, and I've forgiven them. I have placed my trust in people who proved themselves untrustworthy, and I have learned to be more cautious. I have been lead down seemingly "wrong" paths, that ended up being part of the lessons in my journey.

Just like you, I am here to enjoy a human experience (gasp!).

Enough about me. You know a bit more about the woman named Andrea Claire, Psychic Medium.

I have shared with you only a few of the obstacles I have overcome, and some of the joys I have celebrated. When they say what doesn't kill you makes you stronger, I often wonder if I'm made of titanium!

It's time to move on to the "heart and soul" of this book. I will share with you some (but not all) of the stories. Coupled with those stories, I will share some (but not all) of the life lessons I have gathered along the way.

I disconnect with the client when their reading is finished, and will forget the majority of information that came through in their session. This protects us both.

Sometimes there are stories that get carved into my memory because they deeply impacting and simply unforgettable. This book is a collection of some of those stories.

Names have been omitted to uphold confidentiality. If you see yourself in any of these narratives, it is either because it IS your story, or because your story is similar to that of someone else. Every narrative recounted in this book is true.

The life lessons contained within are unsophisticated and incredibly practical. I like to keep things simple. It makes life so much clearer when we do away with complications and drama.

Each chapter intentionally begins with the word "BE". In this fast-paced, "I want it all NOW", "buy buy buy", "snappity snap snap" world we live in, we are becoming human "DO-ings" rather than human BEings.

We need to stop, take a few deep breaths, relax, and take the time to SIMPLY BE.

BE GRATEFUL

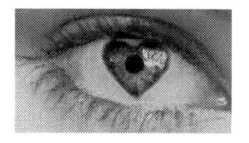

"At times our own light goes out and is rekindled by a spark from another person. Each of us has cause to think with deep gratitude of those who have lighted the flame within us."
(Albert Schweitzer)

The word "gratitude" denotes a deep appreciation of kindnesses and blessings received. When you start being exceedingly grateful for all things in your life – the good stuff and the "not so good" stuff - you will actively increase the perceived value of your existence in this lifetime.

Gratitude comes straight from the heart. It is a powerfully magnetic energy. The "thank you" of gratitude is said with total sincerity.

The frequency with which you think about and express your thanks about, the faster you will start attracting even more wonderful things into your life.

When you start looking at your life as your own masterpiece, and recognize that everything in your life is a direct mirror of whatever thoughts and actions you've "put out there", you might start seeing things differently.

Some of my most poignant lessons in gratitude came in 2007. I supported both my parents on their respective journeys from this life to the after-life. Spending most of that year visiting them in hospitals and nursing homes, I would come home feeling incredibly drained, frustrated, and despondent.

Initially, I definitely was not a happy camper. I knew that I had to find a way to transform these negative days into positive ones. If I didn't make an attempt to elevate my spirit, I somehow sensed that I would become so negative that I would not and could not be of any constructive help to anyone, let alone myself.

Striving to be the eternal optimist, I challenged myself to try to find the silver linings in all of this. By tweaking my perception of the events and environments, I became profoundly affected ... to the extent that my outlooks on life would change forever.

I immediately started viewing my own life in a magical new way.

I knew that my mom and my dad were both going to be passing soon. I became so grateful for the time that we still had together – in whatever capacity – and started reflecting on the many memories we shared in our lives. Simple acts and words of love and appreciation flowed easily for me toward them both. I wanted to be a ray of sunshine in their otherwise gloomy day.

In our daily conversations, my Mom was learning more about me and my past accomplishments. In the past, I usually "played my cards close to my vest" when it came to telling Mom what was going on in my world. She never asked, so I never told. Now I was given an opportunity to share a lot with her.

These times spent visiting Mom in the hospital transformed me on a much deeper level.

All of a sudden, I started appreciating such simple things in my life that I had always taken for granted. Until then, I didn't realize how fortunate I was to be waking up every morning and getting out of my comfortable bed unassisted, being able to walk to my kitchen and make myself a coffee, selecting whatever I wanted to eat for breakfast (rather than being served the hospital's meal of the day), having a soothing warm shower, going to my closet and having an abundance of clothes from which to choose. I had the gift of planning my day in whatever way I chose, and I had the freedom to go wherever I wanted, to see whomever I wanted. My list of blessings continued!

These are all things that we presuppose, and most of us don't recognize the gifts we are presented with each day. Have you ever stopped to think about things like that? It's astonishing!

We complain when the WIFI goes down and we cannot access the internet. Do we appreciate every time that it's up and running and easily accessible?

We complain when the car breaks down, but never think to express our thanks for every time it runs smoothly. Some people don't even realize how fortunate they are to even own an automobile.

We might get down on our knees and pray to God for help in difficult times, but how many of us get down on our knees to convey our gratitude during the good times?

Instead of waiting to recite my prayers of thanks at bedtime, I found myself expressing my thanks to God and the Universe in the moment. This grew into a fun little game, and helped me lighten up. It was mind-blowing when I shifted my focus and started seeing everything for which I am (and should be) truly grateful.

This newfound "attitude of gratitude" also positively affected my relationship with my son. Rather than getting angry when we disagreed over an issue, I started appreciating the fact that I raised a son who was strong-willed, opinionated, and unafraid to speak his truth. He was pushing me to change how I looked at things, and many times I found merit in his words! Sometimes he was MY teacher!!!

We need to witness the contrast in order to appreciate what we have. Interestingly, it seems that whenever we are feeling particularly sorry for ourselves, we are shown something or someone else who has it far worse than we do. Open your eyes and see for yourself!

Do you scoff at the homeless person, or do you feel compassion toward him/her? Do you wonder what happened in their life to result in them becoming homeless? Does it make you feel thankful that you have a roof over your head, food in your tummy, and a safe place to sleep each night?

Does seeing someone in a wheelchair or struggling with crutches make you feel grateful for your own mobility?

Every situation and person in your life serves a purpose. Everyone has a story. Don't ever presume that you've already read theirs.

I can almost hear you saying, "Yeah okay, but what about the other stuff in my life that isn't so enjoyable? How am I supposed to be grateful for my debts, or for that person who hurt my feelings, or for my marriage that fell apart?"

The Wise Ones have told me time and time again: The poignant life lessons don't come when we are in a perpetual state of bliss.

The challenges that are placed before us are designed to TEST us, and TEACH us, and STRETCH us, thereby assisting us in becoming stronger, better, and truer versions of self.

Learning to find those silver linings in situations takes a lot of practice. Search hard enough, and practice long enough, and I guarantee that you will find them.

I had a client sit with me one day, and he was complaining about what had happened "**to** him" the night before. He was racing home on the highway, motoring along at 130 km/h. He exited on the ramp toward home and (insert "grumble sound" here), he heard a "thunk thunk" sound. He realized that his tire had just gone flat. He was almost home, was running late, and now had to deal with this major inconvenience?!?!?!

Without even hesitating, I replied, "Wow, I'd be SO grateful that you were that close to home when you got a flat tire. Imagine what would have happened if you were going 130 km/h on the highway when that tire blew? Gees! You could have been in a serious collision. Or even worse, you could have been killed. If that faulty tire was going to flatten, it couldn't have happened at a better time and place for you."

He paused for a moment, and then smiled. He hadn't looked at it that way, and he thanked me for giving him that perspective.

Things break down. Life happens. I believe that, for the most part, things happen FOR us, not TO us.

When you view life through the eyes of gratitude, some of life's little inconveniences just don't seem that troublesome anymore. Stop complaining! Adjust your perception of the event, and figure out what hidden gifts it contains.

There is much more to life than what you think you see!

Remember those 3-D posters that were popular a while ago? On first glance, you saw a picture that was appealing. However, when you relaxed your eyes and continued to look at the picture, things would get blurry. All of a sudden something different would pop out in the picture!

The same is true when you approach everything from a place of gratitude. When you challenge yourself to look at your life through grateful eyes, the blessings in that picture will pop out in totally unexpected and incredible ways!

If you don't like who you're with, where you live, your job, your friends, the nosy neighbours, the miserable woman at work, etc etc, then take the necessary steps to CHANGE YOUR SITUATION!!!

Change is easier to say than to do. The word itself is both a noun and a verb. Regardless of how you use the word in a sentence, change denotes the movement from one state to a different one.

I have faith in you! I know you can change! It's not that difficult!

For starters, why not count your blessings instead of counting sheep at bedtime? Aren't you fortunate to be curling up in your warm bed, safe and cozy, with a roof over your head? Not everyone has that luxury. Say thank you!

Maybe you had a particularly rough day. But you got through it. Say thank you!

Think about something positive that happened to you that day. If you have to dig really deep, perhaps you could consider something like "At least I didn't get in a car accident today." Say thank you! Think about everything that went RIGHT for you.

An attitude of gratitude will practically guarantee you having sweet dreams!

I have a magnet on my refrigerator that says: TO HAVE MORE, DESIRE LESS. It keeps me in check.
Don't focus on what you **think** you lack. Focus on everything you already have. You are SO blessed. Your cup overflows!

I'm not asking you to wear rose-coloured glasses for

the rest of your life, but I am challenging you to start figuring out the reasons that events and people have been summoned into your life. What purpose do they serve? What can you learn from them? What can you teach them?

Look at everything and everyone who has "written on your soul" from an analytical point of view.

In doing so, you will start becoming more thankful for everything and everyone in your life RIGHT NOW!

"Develop an attitude of gratitude, and give thanks for everything that happens to you, knowing that every step forward is a step toward achieving something bigger and better than your current situation."
(Brian Tracy)

BE OPEN-MINDED

"A mind is like a parachute. It doesn't work if it is not open."
(Frank Zappa)

The term synchronicity can be defined as an apparently meaningful coincidence in the timing of two or more similar or identical events that are causally unrelated".

For the record, I do not believe in coincidence. When you unabashedly chalk things up to "coincidence", then you fail to see the many magical ways that the Universe works FOR you!

I have trained myself to see hidden meaning and messages behind most things in life.

To me, synchronicity is an "angel wink" from the Universe. When amazing things occur and you're left scratching your head and asking, "What were the odds of that happening!?", then you have just experienced a synchronicity.

Have you ever thought about someone out of the blue, and then they call you? Or you surprisingly meet up with them when you're "out and about" (as we Canadians are apparently so famous for saying)? That's synchronicity!

Here's a cute example of a day when I showed up at the **right** place at exactly the **right** time...

I went out with a bunch of errands to run. I mentally pre-planned my course of action, and intended that my final stop would be at the grocery store where my son worked.

My errands took a longer than I expected, and I was an hour behind my "previously planned" schedule. For someone like me, that can be an absolute nightmare! I am very mindful of time and schedules.

When I finally arrived at the grocery store, I was delighted to see my son standing directly at the doors leading into the store. Wow, talk about nice timing! We had a little chat before I went inside to do my shopping.

I intended to go directly to the coffee aisle first, but my gut said, "Go to the produce section."

When I receive a clear intuitive message like that, I love acting on it to see what happens. I'm such a kid at heart!

I went over to the produce section, and was standing by the potatoes, for whatever reason (I didn't really need potatoes!) A lady was coming toward me and almost hit me with her cart. I looked at her, and my jaw dropped. It was a friend of mine who I hadn't seen in over two months, simply because our calendars didn't jive. She was holding down two jobs at the time, and her schedule was beyond tight.

We both said at the same time, "OMG I can't believe this!"

We laughed and caught up on each others news, and set a firm date to meet up for breakfast later that week. Afterwards I appreciated how crucial the timing was in order to orchestrate our meeting. Maybe I really wasn't running late at all. I certainly arrived at the exact perfect place and time to reconnect with my friend!

There were also a series of synchronistic events that pushed me to finally write this book.

For weeks, I had been repeatedly receiving messages from my Guides that I should start working on that "creative project" that I had been postponing. My Guides and I have a solid relationship built on mutual trust and respect, but we also like to have fun too. Sometimes I will push them as hard as they push me.

I *thought* I knew what they were referring to, but I

challenged them to send me some CLEARER signs. Oh boy, did they ever deliver them within a matter of hours!

First, an old friend who I hadn't heard from in over two years emailed me. He told me that he was about to publish a book, and had written a chapter about me being his Spiritual Teacher. Me?!?! He wanted me to "approve" the content that he had written. I thanked and congratulated him and asked him to go ahead and send me that chapter.

His next email contained that chapter for me to approve. He also asked if I had written my book yet.

I replied that I hadn't written my book.

I looked upward, gave a thumbs up, and said to my Guides, "Good one. Thanks for that subtle hint."

I started thinking that perhaps my Guides were saying that it WAS time to focus on writing this book.

When contemplating change, I am like a lot of people. I started to dither. I think I inherited the dither gene from my mom!

A whole bunch of silly fears arose. My "monkey mind" started conjuring up tons and tons of excuses about why I shouldn't or couldn't do this.

What the heck would I write about? How do I get it published? Could I really do this? SHOULD I really do this? I even dug up a memory of a man I once dated saying to me, "Why would you write a book??? Who even cares about what you have to write about?" Ouch!

Clearly, I needed a good swift kick in the butt. And Spirit has a loving way of delivering those kicks when they have to.

In their special way, Spirit pushed the envelope one step further. About half an hour later, an email arrived in my inbox. The message started out …

Are you receiving signs to take creative endeavors or are you seeking guidance to share your passion and vision with the world? Archangel Gabriel is a messenger of God and the patron saint of communication workers. Gabriel opens the door of opportunity for you to work in your chosen career, and gives you a loving push through it if you hesitate. Gabriel helps earthly messengers such as teachers, counselors, writers, artists, and actors.

I KID YOU NOT!!!! I giggled and thought, "Well done, my friends. That was a much clearer sign!" Talk about fantastic timing, too!

My eyes are "trained" to see the magic and synchronicity in life, and I gave Spirit credit for what they accomplished. Messages received! I winked right back at them and said, "Okay, I get it. I'll start writing".

I sat down at my computer, poked around a bit, and realized that I had already built a solid framework for this book years ago. All that I needed to do was fill in the proverbial blanks. I started clicking away on the keyboard.

When the solution is simple, God is answering!

Synchronicity is our Guides' and Angels' way of getting us to lighten up. Bear in mind that our Wise Friends on the Other Side have an amazing sense of humour, (which is probably why I get along with them so well) and they truly give us a boost by sending us messages at the EXACT time that we need them.

A few years ago, my Guides impressed on me that I needed to add some Vitamin B to my diet. (Yes, they will send me messages like that and then I do act on them.) So off to the pharmacy I went, to buy myself some Vitamin B. I went to the vitamin section, and was overwhelmed at the number of different types of Vitamin B on the shelf!

I decided that I had better do a little more research before making the purchase. Besides, I was pressed for time that day. I had to teach a class at the local community center in thirty minutes.

When I arrived at the community center, there was a lady in the room setting up the chairs and tables for my seminar. We started chatting and then, out of the blue, she said, "Andrea, I don't know why I'm telling you this, but you need to buy some Vitamin B12".

She thought she was losing her mind when she shared with me that piece of information. I just smiled and thanked her. When I explained that I had indeed been looking for that answer, she was a little dumbfounded. My Guides had used her as the messenger to deliver the information I required!

THESE COOL THINGS HAPPEN! And not just to me!

Start paying closer attention to what is going on around you. Signs and messages are everywhere. You need to open your eyes and ears. You also need to learn how to decipher the codes!

One day, a lady called and booked a session with me. When we met in person, she told me the "crazy" story that lead her to contacting me.

She was thinking about going to a Psychic to get a reading, and was searching for one on her computer. My website was the first to pop up. She thought that was interesting, but dismissed it, and continued to google around. She went to click on a different website and, again, my website came up instead. Hmmm.

After the third time this happened to her, she finally decided that it must be some sort of "sign", and she gave me a call.

I assure you that I am not capable of making surreal things like that happen. But our Guides and Loved Ones are able to tamper with electronics and can intercept in order to point you in the right direction.

Another client confessed that she wanted to book an appointment with a psychic, and telephoned me because – for some reason – my name "Andrea

Claire" made her heart skip a beat. YAY!

Open your mind and retrain your eyes, and expect to see miracles every day.

When I talk about our Guides communicating with number sequences, a lot of people are startled to confess that it happens to them as well. Do you see patterns like 111 or 222 or 333 (or whatever combo) often? Have you taken the time to google the significance? I won't give away the meanings. Google "spirit number meanings" and figure it out for yourself! Experience your own little "aha moment"!

In a session with a client, I connected with her deceased Uncle. At that time, my client was going through a lot of HUGE changes in her life, and wanted certainty that her Uncle was looking out for her from the Other Side. He assured her that he definitely was helping, and told her that he will start sending her dimes as a sign that he is with her.

From that day forward, she started finding so many random dimes that she became known to her friends and family as the "dime girl". While on a commuter train to Toronto one morning, she was thinking about a legal matter she was facing. By the time she arrived at Union Station (in Toronto), she had finally made an important decision concerning the direction she would take.

She exited the train, looked down on the ground, and found a shiny dime. Let me add that Union Station is an extraordinarily BUSY place – especially during rush hour. What are the odds that she would find a dime at the exact time and exact place that she did? It gave her pause for thought.

The dimes continued to randomly appear, and she felt so confident that her Uncle really was guiding her and supporting her.

Her major "blow me away" moment kind of blew me away too …

She had bought a new home. On moving day, her parents came over to help her clean and unpack. One of her parents did all the vacuuming, and didn't notice any strange noises while doing so. But when they went to empty the vacuum canister, they found a handful of dimes inside.

I love that story!

Start making note of things that seemingly happen "out of the blue" to you.

Do you arrive at the right place at just the right time?

Do you think about someone, and then they get in touch with you?

Are there recurring number patterns that you see on license plates, billboard signs, cash register receipts, or on the clock? (like 111, 222, 333, 1234, etc)?

Listen to what that stranger says to you. Is he/she

imparting a message with solutions that you needed to hear?

Be open-minded and I guarantee that you'll start to experience synchronicity! When you do, then your life becomes almost like a treasure hunt!

Signs and symbols are all around, and helping hands are just around the corner.

Every one of you has Guides and Loved Ones on the Other Side who are working with you and on your behalf. Ask them to start sending you clear signs of their presence. Discard your expectations of how they will amaze you, and instead watch for patterns and synchronistic surprises!

> "Look up at the stars and not down at your feet. Try to make sense of what you see, and wonder about what makes the universe exist. Be curious."
> (Stephen Hawking)

BE DISCERNING

"Love all, trust a few, do wrong to none."
(William Shakespeare)

We are all gifted with intuition, or "gut feelings". Intuition is our internal "GPS" system that, if we trust and follow it, will help to navigate us through this maze in life.

In order to hear your intuitive voice, you have to slow down and be really quiet. You might have to engage in a practice that allows you to calm your mind. Meditate! Go for a walk! Sign up for Yoga classes! Work out at the gym! A lot of people don't understand the importance of making this investment in themselves.

It's an unbelievably noisy world we live in. People are easily distracted by flashy marketing schemes that promise that their product or idea will "make your life so amazing". They'll buy into the latest greatest gizmo that guarantees their instant happiness. They accept someone's truth as their own, without even bothering to test it.

One thing I cannot emphasize enough is the importance of being discerning. What might be beneficial for one person may not be for you. If something doesn't feel "right" to you, then dig in, do some research and figure out why! People are becoming so lazy these days and they are allowing other people to do their thinking on their behalf. Test things! Discover your **own** truth!

This is a planet of contrast. There is good and bad, the dark and the light. It is unfortunate that there are con artists in this world, who seize the media's attention and negate all the good people who are doing honest work in the same field. How many times have you seen headlines about fraudulent doctors, lawyers, and business people, for example?

Psychics and Mediums are also attacked for being scammers, probably because we deal with the intangible, the invisible, the matter that can't be scientifically proven (although Science is finally validating the credibility of psychic phenomenon).

There are those who will PRAY FOR you (like me!), and those who will PREY UPON you. Be careful!

I crossed paths with a gentle lady, who came to me in dire straits. She had met with a known psychic in this area., because she desperately wanted to find help for her brother (who allegedly was terminally ill). This Psychic "read into" the situation and almost immediately determined that the lady's brother was extremely sick because he had a "curse" on him.

How fortuitous for the lady (I hope you detect my sarcasm) ... this Psychic could remove that curse for $1000. Desperate to receive help for her brother, the lady got a cash advance on her credit card and handed the money over to the Psychic.

The Psychic gave her strict instructions, including the fact that this lady was not to breathe a word to anyone that she had consulted with this her, nor was she ever to tell anyone the price of this miraculous cure that she was whipping up. The lady was to return in a week's time for an follow-up visit.

Well, as it turns out, after that week whatever lotion or magical potion that this Psychic concocted didn't work. The brother's health did not change at all.

Upset, the lady went back to see the Psychic. Believe it or not, the Psychic came up with some lame excuse. She accused the lady of either telling people about the treatment she had purchased on behalf of her brother. The lady swore she hadn't. The Psychic concluded that her brother must have done something "wrong" while the potion was administered, thus rendering it ineffective.

If the lady coughed up another $1000, the Psychic said that this next potion would definitely work.

At this point, the lady realized she was being conned and threatened police action if her money wasn't returned. The police wouldn't get involved because the lady had handed over her money willingly. Unreal!

As this lady recounted her story to me, I was both saddened and angry that someone would prey upon her kindness.

If you believe something to be real, then it is real in its consequences. Her brother wasn't cursed. But his "belief" that he was cursed was manifesting into a self-fulfilling prophecy. He had to change his thinking, and make a few other significant modifications to his diet. He did so and I am happy to say that, to this day, he remains healthy.

That Psychic has since skipped town, leaving behind a lot of disillusioned and angry people. She taught us all some crucial lessons. Between us, I don't even want to think about that Psychic's karma!!

I will go on record saying that curses are a bunch of nonsense. Absolutely NO ONE can create ANYTHING in your life without your permission. If you believe you are cursed, then your thoughts will keep creating events to validate this.

Our thoughts shape the experiences we have and the world in which we live. Whatever thoughts you put out there, come right back at you quickly! I know it sounds too syrupy sweet, but it's simply true ... change your thoughts and you can change your life!

I had a client call me on behalf of her friend who was in deep trouble. She didn't give me any details, and wanted me to counsel her friend. Moreover, she was willing to pay for my time on her friend's behalf.

You've probably heard stories similar to the one I am about to tell. It rattled me to the core that I would actually sit in the company of a woman who was the victim of an internet phishing scam.

This lady was a bit older, admittedly very lonely, and was searching online for a mate. She met a man who said all the right things to her, and she was totally enchanted with him! They kept in constant communication for over three years. But they had never met in person.

There was a big hurdle that prevented them meeting. Allegedly, this man was imprisoned in some foreign land, and couldn't post bail. He swore he was innocent. All he needed was for her to post his bail, get him a lawyer, and as soon as this whole mess was straightened out, he promised he would come to Canada and marry her.

She did everything he asked her to do, each and every time he asked her for another small favour.

Over the course of three years, more and more crises arose for this man. Over the three years, she cashed in all of her savings, including her retirement investments, in order to help him. She sold her house and had to move in with her son. Her friends and family pleaded with her to stop this insanity, but she wouldn't listen. She truly believed that this man loved her, as she loved him.

She had sent this man close to $500,000 when all was said and done. He *still* hadn't come to Canada, and they hadn't yet met in person.

Her pressing question for me was, "When do you see us getting married?"

Talk about an awkward moment! It was difficult for me to be the one to put the final nail in this coffin. I told her that she was being conned, that this was a phishing scam, and she would never meet him in person.

She refused to hear that piece of information. In her mind, everything would sort itself out in time, and insisted that they would be happily married one day.

Again, I had to to tell her that it wasn't going to happen.

She justified her actions, telling me that that he promised that he would pay back every cent she had sent him once they got together. I shook my head and told her that her money was gone, and would never be returned.

Apparently she heard me that time. She became extremely angry and immediately dismissed me and the counsel I gave.

In spite of my best efforts to awaken her to this bitter reality, she wouldn't pay attention. I told her to search her heart of hearts and listen to the advice that everyone was giving her, myself included. I was a stranger with no prior knowledge of what was happening to her, and yet I tapped in with precision.

About a month later, this woman contacted me. I was surprised to hear from her, and honestly hoped that she had "seen the light".

Instead, she asked me if I would send her $5000. She was financially tapped out, no one else she knew would give her money, and this man allegedly needed $5000 more in order to come to Canada.

I had to say no to her. Tough love isn't easy. In my heart of hearts, I absolutely could not enable her in this drama. I haven't heard from her since. I hope that she found some sort of resolution.

Where there is a will, there is a way. Dark souls like this man will prey on the kindness of others. Don't enable them. Turn and walk away.

Be aware. Be conscious. Be discerning!

> "Discernment is not a matter of simply telling the difference between right and wrong; rather it is telling the difference between right and almost right."
> (Charles Spurgeon)

BE PRESENT

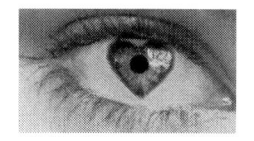

"Do not dwell in the past, do not dream of the future, concentrate the mind on the present moment."
(Buddha)

This is where I reveal to you my "cave woman" values and beliefs. Please don't get me wrong. I like technology! I love the fact that we can connect to the internet and have access to so much information. I openly admit that Google is my professor! It's fantastic that I can chat with friends all over the world without even picking up my phone. I can watch a sunset in Hawaii, or look at people walking the streets in Dublin, Ireland. All sorts of wonderful experiences are merely a few clicks away.

In being more technologically "advanced", I often wonder if we have lost something priceless in the process.

What ever happened to good old-fashioned conversation?

The other day I was out with a friend, who I hadn't seen in over a month. We are both busy people with hectic schedules, yet we finally "pinned" down an afternoon where we were both available! I was really looking forward to hanging out with him.

We met for coffee, and every few minutes he would interrupt our conversation, check his phone, and reply to the texts he was receiving. His phone was literally blowing up with all the "bing bing bing"'s of incoming texts. He'd send a text, immediately get a reply, then he would reply, and on and on. Then he'd put his phone down, give me about ten minutes of his undivided attention, and then the texting would start again.

Being a kind person, I chose to remain silent for the time being. I was going to rise above it.

When we went out shopping and had a bit of fun, he had left his cellphone in the car.

Upon returning to the car, I was driving and he sat in the passenger seat. Apparently he had missed a lot of text messages. The wildfire texting resumed.

Out of concern, I asked him if whoever was texting had some sort of emergency. He smiled and said, "No."

Because the texting continued, I asked if he had to leave. I was dropping subtle hints. He said he didn't want our day to end quite yet. We found an outdoor patio where there was a live band playing. We bought some gelato. I sat and enjoyed mine, while he balanced his on his knee so he could keep texting. At this point, I was getting annoyed.

I suggested that it might be a good idea to end our time together so he could be with that other person who was occupying his time and thoughts. He wasn't really spending time with me after all!

Some of you might think this was immature, but I will disagree. Can we not put our phones away for an hour or two and converse with the person sitting directly across the table from us?

It bears repeating. **What ever happened to good old-fashioned communication?**

When he was younger, my son and I used to take off on little jaunts to Niagara Falls. There were great deals on hotels, and after a fifteen minute drive, we were in another city with a bunch of fun things to do!!

As a business person, I want to stay on top of my emails when I am away on holidays, and I will book my schedule to fulfill upon my return home. I drag my laptop with me and make sure I have my cellphone and its charger so I won't ever miss a call or email.

I realized that this was egotistical on my part, and not fair to either of us. I truly wasn't going away and having a bit of a holiday with my son, was I? I wasn't recharging my own batteries on vacation if I was more concerned about keeping the laptop and cellphone charged in order to keep up with the business correspondence.

The next time that we went away, I DIDN'T pack my laptop, and I shut my cellphone off for our little getaway. My son was shocked, but happy!

I said, "The world will keep revolving if I take a few days off. Let's go have some fun!" And we did! When we returned home, we were both refreshed and had made some great memories together.

Sometimes you need to shut down the technology and literally go "off the grid".

Being present is important. We miss out on so much in life when we are busy worrying, or thinking about tomorrow, or being angry about what happened yesterday. We aren't even paying attention to what's going on today. Tomorrow is never guaranteed.

Today is a gift. Enjoy today as if your life depended on it. It actually does.

We have become the most "plugged in" and disconnected society. The internet has a lot to do with that. Quite honestly, I don't use social media to air my dirty laundry, or to "tweet" where I am or what I'm doing. I really pay no heed to what is "trending" on Facebook. It's drama. In the grand scheme of things, it has no personal effect on my life.

Cellphones are important tools of technology, but there are inappropriate times to use them. I'm not alone in this opinion. I notice others rolling their eyes at the person gabbing on their phone while waiting in line. I giggled at a sign posted in the bank that said, "We would be happy to serve you after you've finished your phone call". Bravo!

I made a strict policy for myself when I am at the gym. My cellphone is safely tucked away in the locker. I am at the gym to exercise, period. I can reply to texts and voicemail messages when my workout is complete. This way, I am truly using the gym for an entire "mind, body, and soul" workout.

I watch people texting while they are crossing the street. Do you remember that video of the girl at the mall who was so busy texting that she fell into the fountain? Classic! I see people texting or talking on their phones while they are on the road. They are distracted and this affects their driving. This has to stop. Please!

I have a complaint about those earbuds and noise canceling headphones, too.

I will walk down the street, smile and say, "Good morning" to the person that I pass on the sidewalk, and they aren't even aware of my presence. They are in their "earbud land". Everyone seems to be in their own little world these days.

When my son was younger, I forbid him from wearing earbuds when he walked to school. I talked to him about the importance of being aware of his surroundings and being "present" when he walked.

Too many drivers ignore the four-way stops, don't "see" that pedestrian crossing the street, are busy having cell phone conversations or texting while they drive, or forget that their vehicles are equipped with turn indicators! I stressed to him the importance of paying attention to what is going on around him, because chances are that people aren't paying attention to him.

It's a spaced out society we live in.

Being conscious and aware of your surroundings really hit home for me one day when I sat with a lady who was in her mid twenties.

During the reading, her former boyfriend came through to say hello. Apparently they had broken up a few months prior to his passing. Years later, she still welled up at the memories of what had happened.

As an aside, whenever I connect with Loved Ones in Spirit, I will telepathically "interview" them. One question I always ask is how they died, in order to provide my client with a definitive validation that it is truly that loved one in Spirit that is coming through. We ALL remember the manner in which someone passed.

I asked her former boyfriend how he died, and he proceeded to show me a little "movie clip" of him walking along the train tracks (which ironically were directly behind my client's home). I could see a train approaching.

And then the little "movie clip" he was showing me came to an abrupt stop.

I described to her what I was being shown and asked, "Seriously? That's how he died?" She nodded, with tears streaming down her face.

We were both speechless.

As it turns out, the day that this young man died, everyone in the neighbourhood could hear the train blaring its whistle repeatedly.

He was walking along the railroad tracks, wearing a pair of noise canceling headphones. He wasn't present in the real world, and not aware of his surroundings. He didn't hear the train whistle of the oncoming train. He died immediately upon impact.

Be safe! Be careful! Remain present and aware of your surroundings. Ignorance is NOT bliss.

"Ignorance is a voluntary misfortune."
(Nicholas Ling)

BE POSITIVE

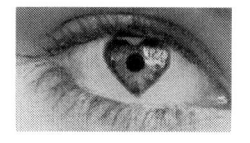

"Keep your face always toward the sunshine and shadows will fall behind you."
(Walt Whitman)

I can't, in good conscience, tell you that a positive outlook will mean that life will ALWAYS be a bowl full of cherries. It won't be. We are constantly being tested. We are always going to be challenged to learn and grow. Things happen. Life happens. The sun isn't going to shine every day.

A positive outlook will, however, determine the manner in which you respond to obstacles that get in the way. How many "tools" do you have in your "tool belt" to solve whatever perceived problems come your way? Perception is everything!!

Every day, we are hit with news about what is going

on in the world. We listen to the latest newscast, scan the feed of what's trending on Facebook, and/or read the daily newspaper. Some of this news can be overwhelming. Things are getting uglier and uglier on this planet. It's tough to be resilient when you're watching a video clip about yet another terrorist attack, for example.

I believe that there is no such thing as "**good news**" or "**bad news**" ... it's all just "**news**".

Our perception of that news – and how we choose to react to it – will determine its impact on us, and ultimately will define how we will view the world in which we live.

There isn't much we can do to change the outcomes of those horrific events. We can hold each other tighter and become more loving to others, though. We can say prayers of gratitude for the life we have. At the end of the day, we are limited in what we can do, other than to stay positive and keep the faith.

One of my University Professors taught me one of my BIGGEST life lessons on the importance of keeping a positive mindset in the midst of pandemonium.

Right smack in the middle of my final exams, in my graduating year, my Mom underwent major surgery in Buffalo, New York. At the same time, my boyfriend's father, who was a workaholic but otherwise a healthy man, suffered a heart attack and literally dropped dead at home. I was a basket case. Having too much stress on my plate, I spoke to my Professor and tried to beg out of writing my final exam. I was an honours student, after all, and I seriously felt that I could be excused based on these extenuating circumstances. Right???

Wrong!

My Professor patiently listened to me babble on, offering excuse after excuse why I couldn't write that exam. He sat quietly, unaffected by my tears.

When I was done with my blubbering, he took a deep breath and said, "Andrea, you have to figure out how to cope with all of this. I believe in you. I will NOT let you out of writing this exam. You must stay positive and discover your strength within."

At that point, I thought I was going to completely lose it. How dare he say that? I was so frustrated!!

But graduating with my Bachelor of Arts degree was very important to me. Seeing that I had no other choice, I re-prioritized my schedule and found time to focus. In the midst of my personal crises, I studied hard. I stayed as positive as I could and summoned as much strength as I could muster.

I received a mark of 85% on that exam.

I will NEVER forget that Professor, and the lesson he taught me that day. I remain so grateful that he showed me the substance I was made of, and how a positive outlook achieves a positive outcome.

I believe that the same great inner strength lies within each and every one of us. You have to find it.

I am very mindful that NO ONE ever comes to me because their life is SO awesome that they can hardly stand themselves. Everyone who sits with me does so because they have reached a crossroad in their life, have experienced their personal definition of "hell", and/or they are looking for guidance.

I remain compassionate and empathetic in listening to their stories. I also learn some bittersweet lessons in the process. I work with them and for them to shed some light on their situations. Without fail, I will leave them with something positive.

A client of mine, whose wife suffered a very painful – but frighteningly fast - death shared his thoughts with me one day.

"Andrea", he said, "I learned that you cannot will yourself to die. But when you lose your will to live, you're done." I will never forget those words, and I agree with him wholeheartedly.

Every morning that we awaken, we are gifted with another opportunity to live our life as we choose.

When you wake up in the morning, do you wake up with a smile? Do you think about what you will do with your day? Who will you lean on, or who will lean on you? What will you learn today? Will you be a "day MAKER", or will you be a "day BREAKER"?

Personally, I create an approximate sketch of my day each morning, and then leave plenty of room to accommodate the "wild cards" that will inevitably arise. Rather than getting stressed out over things that will creep up, I do my best to remain positive.

I also make a conscious effort to leave my clients, no matter what they are facing, with hope. Regardless of what you're going through, you **will** get through it. Things will shift. It will change. Nothing lasts forever.

No one knows what is going on inside your head, unless you speak up. I remember how saddened I was when the comedian, Robin Williams, committed suicide. He devoted his life to making others laugh, and no one knew how much he was hurting inside. Life is fraught with irony, isn't it?

I can't count the number of young people I've counseled, who seem to have it all going on on the exterior, and inside they are an absolute mess! They are so worried about being "just like everyone else", and saying and doing what the others want them to say or do, and they have lost themselves as a result.

Even those who "dare" to be different, who choose to be positive role models, and govern themselves accordingly will be targets for criticism and abuse.

People tend to project their low feelings of self-worth on you. What they say has more to do their internal state of affairs than yours.

Just shrug your shoulders and say, "Hey, thanks for sharing." Then let it go.

Narrow thinking results in narrow-mindedness. Negative attracts more negative. Some people thrive on pessimism. Don't be one of them.

Positive always attracts more positive. Gravitate toward that instead!!

Positive thinking not only shifts your state of being, but also creates real value in your life. Believe in yourself, no matter what others may say to the contrary.

Life really IS all about YOU and the choices you make.

> "Let us rise up and be thankful, for if we didn't learn a lot today, at least we learned a little, and if we didn't learn a little, at least we didn't get sick, and if we got sick, at least we didn't die, so let us all be thankful."
> (Buddha)

BE ACCEPTING

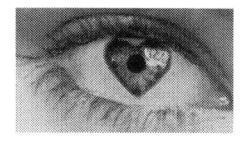

"God, grant me the serenity to accept the things I cannot change, courage to change the things I can, and wisdom to know the difference."
(from the Serenity Prayer, Reinhold Niebuhr)

How many times do we get frustrated in attempting to force a square peg into a round hole? No matter how hard we try, or how many attempts we make, that peg just isn't going to fit in that hole.

As well, we try to "own" circumstances, people, etc that are NOT ours to own. Some will take on partners with the intention of "fixing" the things they don't like about them. Some take on others' problems that are not theirs to resolve, and end up feeling frustrated, disheartened, and exhausted when things **still** don't work out the way that THEY had intended.

I'm going to lift a two thousand pound weight off your shoulders ...

We are simply the CARETAKERS of those we love. We are not their owners.

We are not supposed to own their actions, to own their problems, or to own their lives. We are not responsible for their personal happiness. We can contribute to it, but ultimately it's THEIR choice to be happy or unhappy.

We cannot change people. We can inspire them to change, through our own actions. We can lend a hand, but not continue to bail people out of We are meant to teach, guide, support, counsel, and uplift.

This does not imply that we should turn our backs on those in need. Instead, we should help those who require assistance. We should lend them a hand, but never a hand-out. Teach them how to do better! Show them the way!

We cannot take everything off others' plates. Who do we think we are, trying to prevent people from learning their own lessons? Do we even have the right to do that? I don't think so!

For example, if someone you love is undergoing surgery, it is impossible for you to jump on that operating table on their behalf. You could pray, support, keep that person comfortable, and take really awesome care of him/her while they recovered. You could provide food, pick up prescriptions, ensure that they take the proper dose of medication to aid in healing. You could drive them to the pre-op and post-op appointments. In short, you can do absolutely everything imaginable to support and care for them during this time, but this is the only power you have to affect the situation.

One of my common expressions is "People plan, and God laughs". I have learned, witnessed, and accepted that there is always a Divine plan in order. That plan isn't necessarily what **we** think it should be.

When you're sitting in the middle of a crisis, the last thing you want to be told is that everything is unfolding as it should, for the highest and greatest good of all. Nor do you want to hear that everything will be just fine, without some sort of tangible proof.

There definitely is a Divine Process in the works, though, and we are all part of its' unfolding. Drop those worries and work on building your faith instead.

Let me talk for a moment about the difference between a "belief" and a "knowing".

A belief is something that we have been told, that we willingly adopt into our belief system, without giving it much thought.

When, however, we go into the world and test that belief over and over again, and find it to be true every single time, then it becomes part of our "knowing". It is carved on our soul, and it shapes our reality.

If someone tells you something that you either believe or don't believe, go out and test it. See how it resonates with you. Either way, you will make it part of your personal code.

Let's get back to this whole concept of control. How do you respond when you think you have lost control of someone or something? How do you feel when you think you could have changed how something unfolded? What happens when something didn't turn out quite the way you "expected" it to? How many times will you beat yourself up with the "woulda coulda shoulda's'"?

When we cannot control a person or a situation, we freak out. We get angry. We go to the place of fear. We try to regain a sense of control. This will afford you a false sense of power.

Fear will shut you down every single time. Stop it! Stop panicking, stop getting angry, and PLEASE stop thumbing your nose at God!!

I think back on a particularly emotional session I had with a client in his mid fifties. During the reading, I connected with and delivered messages from his deceased grandfather. My client burst into tears upon being reconnected with his much beloved grandfather. He desperately wanted to ask him a very important question. Did his grandfather forgive him?

The grandfather let out a guffaw (in a loving way), and told his grandson that he had done nothing wrong. He explained that it was what it was, and no forgiveness was required. At first I felt that was a rather harsh comment, but I was so wrong!

His grandfather waited in silence while my client explained the situation to me. His grandfather was his whole world, and he loved to go visit him almost everyday.

One day, however, ended in tragedy and forever scarred my client. He went over to visit, and was met with the worst news ever. That very day, after his grandfather had finished cutting the lawn, he suffered a massive heart attack, and died immediately.

Through the eyes of a child, my client believed that, perhaps if he arrived earlier, he could have prevented his grandfather's death. Or, even better, if he had come over and **insisted** that he cut the lawn for his grandfather, then none of this would have ever happened.

He carried such guilt and shame, and felt so powerless as life went on. As an adult, he morphed into the classic "rescuer" and control-freak in life in order to atone for his perceived "sin".

I asked my client how old he was when this happened. He was eight.

I asked him if, at age eight, was he well-versed in administering CPR and could he have restarted his grandfather's heart? He said, "No." (and he gave me "DUHH" look, but that was fine with me).

Then I asked if anyone was around who could have called an ambulance. (Back then we didn't have cell phones at our disposal). He explained that when his grandmother got home, she called the ambulance, but it was too late. His grandfather was already dead.

How many times prior to this event had he offered to cut his grandfather's lawn for him? He laughed and said, "Too many times to count, and my grandfather always said 'no'."

I asked him, then, "Then why do you feel you need to be forgiven?"

My client sat without saying a word. I could sense that he was starting to see things differently. He wasn't responsible for his grandfather's death after all! He had done nothing wrong. He didn't require forgiveness. This self-created burden of blame he carried for fifty years could now be dropped.

His grandfather spent the rest of the session recounting happy times that they shared, commenting on the renovations he is watching his grandson currently doing in his own home, and of course imparting loving words of advice. My client laughed and cried as they recalled the "good old days". And his grandfather thanked him for all of the special memories they made together.

I could feel a genuine shift in my client when we ended the session. He was now free to remember his grandfather and all the good memories they created together, and not feel responsible for his grandfather's death.

The decision to part this world rests between God and the person on their deathbed. It's **their** contract - not ours - to negotiate. You have no power to affect change in this matter.

Have you heard stories about the family taking a break from their vigil? They left the hospital room to get a coffee and a bite to eat, and their loved one died while they were downstairs in the cafeteria.

Have you heard accounts about someone delaying their passing until a family member arrived to visit with them? Shortly after they arrive, the person dies.

They will pass at whatever time that they feel is appropriate for them to do so, regardless.

I am also able to connect with people who are still alive, but are either in a coma, in advanced stages of Alzheimer's or suffering from dementia. Please know that, although they are appear to be unresponsive, on a soul level they are very much aware of what is happening. They hear all, and see all.

I sat with a client one day, and brought through her father. He was actually still alive, but was battling a terminal disease. For the most part, he slept. I must have connected with him while he was napping.

He gave her enough validations so that she knew that it was indeed her father coming through.

He was aware that there was a power struggle between her and her sister, and it was making things awkward and difficult for everyone. Her sister was argumentative and micromanaging everything and destroying what little time he had remaining.

Then he told her that he was going to die peacefully in his sleep while her sister was away in the United States. He felt that it would be easier for everyone.

She looked at me in shock, and told me that her sister was going for a short vacation in the United States the following weekend.

I shrugged my shoulders, and assured her that her father was aware of what was going on.

Sure enough, he kept his word. She called me the following week to let me know that her father died on the weekend that her sister went away. It brought her a sense of peace knowing that this was exactly what her Dad had planned.

Those who are close to death will choose their exit point. When they are satisfied that they have completed whatever it is they want to complete, they will pass away.

When I supported my Mom in her journey from this life to the afterlife, I hit a point where I didn't know how to pray for her anymore. Mom was struggling. It was difficult to watch.

Should I pray to God to keep her here, in a state of disease and discomfort, because I felt that was how it should be? Or should I pray to God to put Mom out of her misery? Do I ask Him to take her home? Do I pray for one last miracle? I didn't have the answers.

For whatever reason that my Mom was sticking around in this condition, it wasn't mine to own. It was a powerful feeling in accepting that I couldn't control this situation. Did I really think that I could play the role of God here?

Reluctantly and bravely, I recognized that things were going to unfold in their own time and in their own way.

I had no say whatsoever in the matter. My only prayer became, "Thy will be done".

A week prior to her passing, I went to visit her at the nursing home, as was my daily routine. She was bright, alert, and sitting up in bed with a huge smile on her face. This was a welcome change! She couldn't wait to tell me her exciting, fantastic news.

She told me that she had had a conversation with God the night before, and she had begged him for more time. She wasn't ready to pass yet. She was so delighted to have been granted more time!

I was so happy for her (and for me!). But I explained to her that it would take a bit of time for her physical body to catch up with her mental decision to stay around. For months and months, she hadn't eaten and wasn't strong.

I encouraged her and said, "Be patient!!"

Our visits changed after her talk with God. Normally bedridden, she insisted on being placed in a wheelchair. She and I went to the cafe in the nursing home and indulged in coffee and cheesecake. Yum!

The next day she went to the hair salon in the nursing home and had her hair and nails done! (I had never ever seen my mom wearing nail polish. This was quite the jolt!!)

Over the course of a few days, she participated in other activities. She went to a church service, and she even played bowling (while in her wheelchair!).

It was an amazing and memorable time for both of us.

Things started turning on the fifth day. In spite of her desire to live, her body was not supporting her choice. She went downhill quickly. She was very tired and depressed. I sensed that her battle was almost over. It broke my heart to witness this.

The day before she passed, we had a heartfelt chat. She told me that she had made a big mistake. She didn't want to stick around after all. All I could say was,"I understand, Mom. You need to do what you need to do."

She accused me of wanting her to die. I told her that she was wrong. All that I ever wanted was for her to be at happy and at peace. If this meant that she was choosing to die, then I would have to figure out how to live in this world without my Mom in it.

From this conversation, I knew she had made her choice. Her death was imminent.

As an aside, throughout the year, I kept praying to God and BEGGING Him to arrange the circumstances so I WASN'T there when Mom took her final breath. I negotiated with Him. I promised I would visit Mom every day. I would try to feed her, I would try to be the best daughter ever!!

"But please, God", I begged, "**don't** make me be there to witness her last breath." I honestly believed that I wouldn't be strong enough to handle being there as she took her last breath.

People plan and God laughs. There WAS a Divine plan in order.

The circumstances surrounding my Mom's death couldn't have been more perfectly scripted and designed so that I COULD BE and WAS PRESENT on that fateful day. If I relayed to you all of the finely tuned details surrounding her death, you would be shocked. I still am. But I won't go into it now.

Mom passed with me by her side, holding her hand. It still brings tears to my eyes when I think about it. And it also makes me realize that I had been gifted with an experience that I will never forget.

I recall an elderly gentleman telling me about his wife's passing. She had been diagnosed with cancer, and after many conversations, they decided that (in spite of her age) she would go through with the chemotherapy treatments. He was driving her to her first chemotherapy appointment.

Sitting in the passenger seat, she turned to him and and informed him that she had changed her mind. She didn't want to go through with the treatments after all.

With that, she looked upward, opened her hands in praise, and ... this is absolute truth ... she died that very moment in the car. His story left me in awe.

Please stop trying to own things that are not yours. Be as gentle and kind and loving to yourself as you are to the one who is going through their "whatever". Do your best to support them, relinquish the reins, and trust in the process. Grab and appreciate every moment you are given, and don't worry about tomorrow. It might never come.

You will find great power when you learn to accept those things that are beyond your ability to change. Rather than try to control it, embrace it, appreciate every moment that you have left, and release the burden of blame.

"Life is a series of natural and spontaneous changes. Don't resist them; that only creates sorrow. Let reality be reality. Let things flow naturally forward in whatever way they like."
(Lao Tzu)

BE WILLING TO BREAK A SWEAT

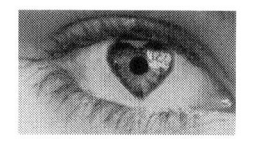

"Knowing is not enough, we must apply. Willing is not enough, we must do."

(Bruce Lee)

What is your wildest dream? Are you stopping yourself from pursuing your dreams because others say they are ridiculous, unattainable, or that it's irresponsible to live in a "dream world"?

As children, we were probably told that if we would be happy when we got a good job, made lots of money, got married, had children, and lived in a big home. Most of us have had these ideologies drilled into us, and made them part of our core belief system.

So we went out, achieved those goals, and found that we were still unhappy. What do we do then?

"They" tell us that dreams are for kids. We need to be practical. "They" believe that if you take a risk, you'll probably fail. "They" say that there's almost nothing more agonizing than failing. What if you view failure not as failure, but as a beautiful life lesson instead?

Who the heck are "They" anyhow? What gives them the right to dictate to us, and impose their will upon us? Why do we listen to them and ignore our soul cry?

I remember a former boss of mine telling me that the louder someone speaks, the more you think they know what they're talking about. I couldn't agree more.

I will concede that we live in a world where money is the currency of exchange. Without a source of income, life can be pretty bleak. Money doesn't necessarily buy happiness, though.

It doesn't mean that you have no choice but to stay in a mundane job where you are unhappy. Wouldn't you rather earn a living by doing something you absolutely love doing instead?

Have you searched your heart of hearts to define what your version of "happy" looks and feels like?

Do you know what would bring you great joy, but you keep talking yourself out of doing it? Is there a creative side within you that needs to be expressed?

WHAT IS **YOUR** WILDEST DREAM?

When you do something that you're passionate about, the money will always follow you. Don't make money your motivator, because I guarantee you that you will never ever have enough.

HERE IS THE HONEST TRUTH: You are a powerful creator. In order to bring your dream to fruition, you have to break a sweat. Each day, you have to take inspired action to push that dream forward! You have to behave according to your vision, and not in a manner that's counterproductive to achieving that dream.

It's not about "talking the talk". It's about WALKING your talk, and not necessarily "talking" about it while you're walking it. It takes a lot of pressure off you if you just quietly go about achieving your dreams without advertising them to others.

Last year, I set a personal goal to lose weight and get healthier. Admittedly I wasn't doing a lot to support achieving that goal. I wasn't counting my calories, and I wasn't exercising. Basically I wasn't acting in a manner that would help me to lose those pounds. It was unrealistic to think that I could just lie on the sofa, envision myself at the weight I wanted to be, and let it go at that. I had to take action!

I joined the gym. But there was more involved than just signing a contract and paying the monthly fees.

It's one thing to have the gym membership tag dangling on my key chain as some sort of status symbol. That tag was worthless unless I actually WENT to the gym.

When I went to the gym, I couldn't just stand around and watch everyone else working out. I had to jump right in, hop on the treadmill and BREAK A SWEAT!!!!!

To date, I have lost weight. I don't weigh myself. My rule of thumb is if my clothes are loose, I lost weight. If they're tight, I gained weight. So far so good!

I don't brag about my accomplishments. I stay focused and quietly plug away. Whether people notice or not, I am unaffected by their reactions (or lack thereof!) All that matters is that I believe in myself and that I will achieve my goal.

> "Whether you think you can, or you think you can't--
> you're right."
> (Henry Ford)

I do my very best to be a cheerleader for others. Nothing makes me happier than to emotionally boost someone who is working toward fulfilling their dream, and then to witness that dream become their reality.

In chasing your dreams, you will meet a new cast of characters in your life. You will quickly discover who are your friends, your enemies, and your "frenemies".

Your true friends are the ones who will root you on through thick and thin. They believe in your success. They will say whatever needs to be said and do whatever needs to be done to boost you and keep you motivated. They are your helpers. They will lend a hand, but not necessarily a hand-out. They know you can do this! They are just as excited for you as you are!!!

Are you a true friend? Are you inspired by your friends' successes? Are you the one who will throw the congratulatory party to honour their achievement? Will you share their story with other people, because you're so proud of what they've accomplished?

Your enemies will be jealous as they see you start living the life you've dreamed about living. They'll be envious that you're making awesome things happen. They are sitting in their personal funk and doing nothing to change it. They will criticize you for doing what you're doing, and try their darnedest to stop you in your tracks. They don't want you to change, because they might lose you in the process. Or, even worse for them, it would reveal that they can change their own life too.

Your enemies are actually projecting their insecurities and negativity on you. Don't pay them any attention. Don't buy into it.

Your "frenemies" pretend to care about you, and will want to hear all about what's going on in your life. But they're just gossip mongers who smile in your direction, feigning their support. They may promise to help you, and later come up with an excuse about why they couldn't after all. What they are really doing is gathering ammunition, and will use it to talk negatively about you behind your back. They're secretly hoping that you will fall flat on your face.

You have all probably heard about the Law of Attraction – the Universal law stating that you attract into your life that which you are. I will not go into a lengthy commentary about the Law itself. But I will state the following:

Unless you are clear, specific, and desiring of something that is in the highest interest of all involved, it isn't going to come about.

Ask yourself why you want to achieve your goal.

Here's a classic "Andrea" example: I was going to teach a workshop on Conscious Creation. I reserved and paid for the room, had performed calculations about the number of attendees I required in order to to cover my expenses, and the number of people required in order to generate a bit of an income for myself.

I decided that my magic number was ten people.

I went to the gym (which is also where I "zone out") and launched my request to the Universe. For two consecutive days, I asked for ten or more students to attend the seminar. I would go home expecting to find emails from people wanting to sign up for this class. Instead, there was no response whatsoever.

On the third day I repeated this routine. I also had a heart-to-heart dialogue with my Guides. Why wasn't I getting the required number of attendees for the seminar?

I asked them, "How can I even teach a seminar on Conscious Creation if I can't even consciously create the number of people I require to attend it?" It was a bit frustrating, but sort of funny at the same time.

My Guides responded immediately, asking me, "Why do you want to hold this seminar?"

That was a solid question, not to be taken lightly.

Upon deliberation, I said "I want to educate, empower, and enlighten people. Conscious creation is important. I know we are powerful creators. My hope is to teach others how to effectively use this tool as a means to fulfilling their dreams."

Once I got clear on my intention – that teaching this workshop wasn't about making a profit – but instead about enlightening and educating - the seminar booked to capacity.

I learned a priceless lesson in the process.

Without being clear and specific in defining your goals, it can become very confusing. It's like going grocery shopping without a list. Chances are you'll end up wandering through the aisles, looking at this and looking at that. At the end of the excursion, you probably filled your cart with a bunch of things you didn't really need, you wasted time and energy, probably spent more money than you intended to, and will discover, when you get home, that you forgot the most important thing on your list - to get milk!!!

I have an awesome and intelligent client who was getting more and more frustrated with his job. He was the "brains" behind the company with whom he was employed. And, like most, he was undervalued and underpaid. Every day that he walked into the building, he was frustrated and angry.

We spoke at great length about the prospect of him starting his own business. How would it feel to him to be at the helm of HIS OWN ship, providing the same excellent customer service and expertise to his OWN client base?

He got caught up in envisioning that dream! He could still provide excellent customer service, doing a job that he really loved, all the while earning a decent income, maintaining his own hours and being able to spend more time with his family.

His Guides had a lot to share about the fundamentals about opening his business. They discussed startup costs and how to build the business gradually. They identified the "nice to haves" versus the "need to haves" with respect to capital purchases. They said that eventually there would be a need to hire more staff, but not to worry about that yet. He would initially manage all aspects of the business himself.
The business plan they were presenting to us was brilliant! They even told him how to design his business card, right down to colours and logo!

But then my client's "yeah buts" kicked in. "Yeah, but it's a big financial risk." and "Yeah, but my wife says that I should hold on to my job. It's ridiculous to walk away from a steady income."

Then he asked, "Yeah, but if it doesn't work out?"

I countered with, "Yeah, but what if it does?"

I could clearly see it all, witness his imminent success, and all of the positive changes coming his way.

I said to him, "Even if you can't see your own success, I definitely do. I believe in you!"

We all need people who believe in us and root us on, especially in those times that we question ourselves and our own capabilities.

All of the information he was presented with was logical. Coupled with the encouragement I offered, it seemed to be enough of a push for him. He took the necessary steps and opened his business.

The last time we met, he told me how profitable his business was! In a matter of months, he was already in a position to hire and train new staff.

With a huge smile on his face, he presented me with

his business card (the same colours and logo that his Guides had mentioned), which I keep in my wallet to this day. I couldn't be happier for him!

You need to keep the faith and stop with the "yeah but's". Every time you say "Yeah, but...", you cancel your original statement. Even if you can't see the Higher plan, know that the plan is in place.

Seriously, had anyone told me at the age of twenty that I would get a degree in Sociology, go through some hard life lessons, finally embrace my calling, and have a full-time practice as a Psychic Medium and Counselor, I would have "yeah butted" through that entire prediction. At that point in my life, it would have sounded utterly ridiculous. Thank God that I didn't know back then what I know now!

Manifesting your dreams requires patience and persistence. You will be constantly challenged to determine how much of a sweat you are willing to break in order to achieve your goals.

That expression "fake it til you make it" doesn't sit well with me. Sincerity is key. "Faking it" implies telling lies and/or stretching the truth about who you are and what you've accomplished. Lies breed more lies.

Don't act your way to success. Keep it real. Live instead in honesty and integrity. This way, you don't need to have a good memory!

Always act in accordance with the intention to achieve your dream, and align yourself with people and events that help you bring about its fulfillment.

Ask yourself, "Does what I am being offered or do the people I am hanging out with actually help me toward attaining my goal, or drag me further away from it?". Test this constantly!!

Let's say you have "frenemies" who catch wind of something fantastic that you are working toward. I'd be willing to bet that they will start sidetracking you with other temptations. You will have to learn how to say the word "no" with conviction. You might even have to detach from them, even if it's temporarily!!

What if you're saving money to buy your dream home, and a friend begs you to go on an expensive vacation with them instead? What will you do? Which is more important to you?

What happens when you announce that you're on a diet, and a "friend" shows up at your door with a box of donuts? Are you going to eat those donuts because you don't hurt your friend's feelings?

Set boundaries and learn how to politely say "no". Don't sell your soul to spare someone else's.

When I am working on a particular goal, I like to change my computer passwords to reflect what I want to achieve. It's a fun way to remind yourself. Every time that I type that password, it brings my goal to the forefront of my mind again.

I frequently meet with clients that are literally two inches away from the "finish line" in reaching their goal, and they give up. Call it fear, call it impatience, call it a lack of faith, call it "too much work", call it getting sidetracked, call it whatever you want to call it. They just need that little push to get over the last hurdle.

I delivered a message to a lady who was meant to be honing her psychic gifts and giving readings. Naturally I asked her why she wasn't doing "her work".

She said she felt insecure and didn't think that she could give messages the way I do. I could see that she was a truly brilliant reader, who gave messages in her own special style.

I explained to her that this didn't happen overnight for me. Like me, though, she would have to commit to her path, stay focused, and keep learning from her own Guides. This process unfolds in its own time, and not necessarily her own. She had to keep training.

The difference between good, better, and even much better is practice practice practice!! Keep on keeping on and keep going with the flow.

Stay true to your vision and stick to your goals. Believe in yourself, regardless of what others may say or think. Be willing to break a sweat, and hang in there for the long haul. It will definitely be worth it, and so much more meaningful when you appreciate that you truly earned it!

> "Nothing is *impossible.* The word itself says **'I'm possible**'!"
> (Audrey Hepburn)

BE KIND

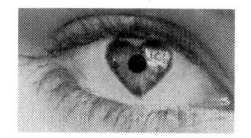

"No act of kindness, no matter how small, is ever wasted."

(Aesop)

Years ago, a friend and I were out at a business networking event. We were both small business owners, and very new at this whole "let's get out and promote our services" thing.

Rather than schmoozing with other business people in attendance, we spent the entire evening chatting with each other. In other words, we stayed in our comfort zone!

The next day she called me and told me that we really need to work on our networking skills, so she signed us both up for a class in public speaking. And she wouldn't hear any excuses from me. We were going to take this class. End of story. Now that's a true friend!

For three hours of time, one evening per week, for ten long weeks we went to this class. I faltered and stammered, and one time I completely "froze" while speaking. Good lessons. I can honestly say that, in spite of it all, I was feeling more and more confident and "polished" as each week passed. We were challenged with something new every week: impromptu speeches, presentations with props, speeches that we had to memorize, etc etc. .

This public speaking course had a bit of a spiritual base. Our final assignment was to write and deliver a speech about one thing we promised to do, from this point forward, as an act of kindness toward others.

This was a challenge I had to seriously think about. What was it that I could COMMIT to doing and about speak with passion?

It took me awhile, and I searched my heart of hearts. Finally I came up with an idea.

On our final evening, we all presented our speeches. Some financial advisers promised to give a client a free consultation per month. Some others promised to tithe ten percent of their earnings to charity. Some promised to volunteer at the food bank once per month.

Awesome stuff!

Then it was my turn to present. The promise that I vowed to uphold for the rest of my life was that each and every day, I would make sure that I smiled at someone. That's it. Plain and simple. I would smile at strangers.

Smiles are absolutely contagious! If you randomly smile at someone, it's almost impossible for them to not return a smile back. I have witnessed people's moods shift when I smile at them.

As well, I always greet a cashier at a store with a smile, making eye contact, and saying "hello". If they respond, and if the store isn't too busy, I'll ask them how their day is going, and actually stand there and listen to their response.

I went shopping at the Mall around Christmas time. This is something I don't normally do, because I really don't like being in that frenetic energy at that time of the year. People are so miserable, rushing around here and there, in and out of stores, bumping into you as if you were invisible!

Anyhow, I went into a store and found the perfect gift for someone on my list. I waited in line for about five minutes before it was my turn to cash out. When I got to the front of the line, I smiled at the cashier, and said "Hi, how are you today?"

She looked up at me, in a bit of a daze. Then she looked at her watch. I expected her to say something like she'd be feeling better in an hour, when her shift was finally over and she could go home and relax.

Instead she said, "It's 2:00pm, and did you know that you are the first person that has even bothered to ask me how my day is going?"

Really? There's something wrong here. People can't take the time to be kind to each another?

Kindness cannot be faked. It comes genuinely from the heart. It's not that drippy type of nonsense. It's honest and direct. A kind person is kind to all, without the hidden motive of "If I am nice to this person, what will I get in return?".

I remember a session with a particularly beautiful teenager. She was a total knockout! She had perfect teeth, shiny thick black long hair, a gorgeous figure, was a straight-A student, was dating the captain of the hockey team, and was living – to some – the dream!

She was also being verbally attacked and bullied by a group of other teenage girls, who constantly slammed her on Facebook and other forms of social media. They made rude comments to her at school. She had no friends. And sadly, she had attempted suicide because of this.

Thankfully it was an unsuccessful attempt.

Her mom sought professional help for her, and her daughter was now being medicated for depression. When I had the honour of sitting with this beautiful young lady, she remained very quiet during the reading.

I had no prior knowledge of anything she had gone through. I tapped into her and all of this information about her life came flowing through.

She nodded at everything I was saying. And I really didn't like relaying the messages I was receiving about what had happened. Messages about the bullying, about her struggles, and about her attempted suicide.

I looked her straight in the eyes, and said, "They are jealous of you. And they have every right to be. You have a very bright future ahead of you. Don't sink to their level."

She started crying. She hadn't been able to see outside of this "prison" the girls had locked her in, and didn't realize the truth in the matter. She had no idea that they actually envied her! She thought there was something inherently wrong with her. I still shake my head when I think about that.

Why do people have to be so cruel? Have we lost our humanity? What is going on?

We have NO right to judge others, even if we **HAVE** walked in their shoes. How dare anyone criticize someone if they cannot even begin to relate to what that person is going through?

The only thing we should be evaluating is our personal reaction to whatever we are witnessing. Leave the judgments of others to Judge Judy and keep your nose out of other people's business!!

A kind person will try to understand and commiserate with others' difficulties.

The higher you rise, the more some will try to take you down. Ignore them and keep going. Continue to raise your bar. Either you will inspire others to do the same, or you'll leave them in your dust.

Be kind to others and be kinder to yourself. People will treat you in the manner that you allow them.

"And every day, the world will drag you by the hand, yelling, 'This is important! And this is important! And this is important! You need to worry about this! And this! And this!' And each day, it's up to you to yank your hand back, put it on your heart and say, 'No. This is what's important.'"

(Iain Thomas)

BE FORGIVING

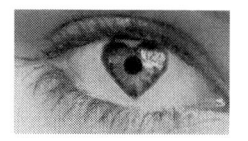

"We must develop and maintain the capacity to forgive. He who is devoid of the power to forgive is devoid of the power to love. There is some good in the worst of us and some evil in the best of us. When we discover this, we are less prone to hate our enemies."

(Martin Luther King Jr)

One of life's greatest challenges is to find peace and forgiveness, and to be at peace and forgiving of all that is, all that was, and all that will be.

To search externally for peace is superfluous. Peace originates from within, and changes how you view life. You cannot find peace in the outside world. You have to CREATE a state of peace inside of yourself.

Every experience, **every** person, **every** place, and **every** thing that is set before us presents us with opportunities to learn, teach, and grow!

Move away from that place of denial, of finger pointing, of playing the "blame game". Each time that you point the finger of blame at someone else, notice that there are three fingers pointing right back at you.

People present the true version of themselves at any given moment. Hey, we're all doing the best that we can! No one is perfect! We all have things to work on and lessons to learn!

I will never forget an experience I had one evening when I was delivering messages from loved ones in Spirit to a group. A mom in Spirit came through, wanting to relay a message to her daughter who was in attendance that night. I approached this woman and told her that her Mom was here and would like to say something to her. She immediately crossed her arms and said something like, "I don't want to hear from that 'b*!*!'. She's dead. It's over."

There was a collective gasp from the group. I said, "Really?"

She said (with arms crossed even tighter), "Tell her to go away. I don't want to hear anything that she has to say."

It didn't take a rocket scientist to see that, whatever had happened between them in the past was still very much present in this woman's mind. The anger she held toward her mom was still eating away at her. Whatever had transpired between them was going to continue gnawing away and negatively affecting this woman's life, until she learned to make peace with it.

I will not deliver a message to someone who refuses to receive one (my integrity!!), but her Mom didn't want to leave! So, her Mom and I telepathically chatted in silence. Her Mom desperately wanted to deliver a sincere apology to her daughter, and ask for her forgiveness. Her Mom told me that she couldn't see the errors of her ways when she was alive, and was now seeing the situation from a higher perspective. I refer to it as "the bird's eye view".

I commiserated with that Mom in Spirit, sent her my love, thanked her for trying, and reluctantly "hung up the line" without relaying her message. How unfortunate.

This was a lost opportunity for two souls to reconnect, to make peace, to resolve their issues, for that daughter to drop her anger and resentment, and move forward much lighter as a result.

People get so stuck in being "right" that they become righteous in their rightness! They refuse to bend, or listen to alternate points of view.

There are always three sides to every story … your side, their side, and somewhere in between lies the actual truth.

It's easier to resolve conflict with people when they are still alive, rather than wait until they cross over and then call in a Medium to talk to their loved one. Forgiveness heals everyone involved.

If someone ticks you off, address it. Don't let things build and fester inside of you. If you're angry or disappointed with someone, talk it out and resolve it! And if you love someone, let them know!

If, for whatever reason, you cannot make peace with someone, then make peace with what transpired between the two of you.

If that person abruptly left you and triple-bolted the door behind them, then own your part in it, be grateful for having known them, and be thankful that it's over.

Forgive them, take the lessons from the experience (because the lessons are **always** there), and use these lessons to move forward.

Challenge yourself to do this with every relationship you've had in life. Try to see what role the key players have played, and figure out what you learned from them.

Some actions against others are clearly painful and unforgivable. If you can't forgive the act, try to forgive the person for not knowing better.

I had a life-changing conversation with my father before he died. I found a way to forgive my father for the role he played, or more precisely, that he DIDN'T play in my life.

Dad had never been a "dad" for me in the truest sense of the word. My Mom and Dad bitterly divorced when I was in grade six, and from that point forward, the only time we spent with Dad was per "court ordered" visitation. Our meetings were always strained and uncomfortable.

He was an absentee parent, and I learned to overcome the reality.

In his final years, Dad was living in a nursing home. I would sporadically drop in to visit him, and our conversations always lacked depth. He would thank me for coming in, and then send me on my way.

His wife called me one day and informed me that Dad's health was deteriorating quickly. I canceled my plans and went in to pay him a visit. Seeing Dad became my top priority that day.

I entered his room and he was awake. My Stepmom and my Aunt left the room so Dad and I could have a little private time together.

An oxygen mask prevented Dad from talking to me. I sat beside him on his bed as he laid there, and quietly did all the talking.

I thanked him for being the PERFECT father for me. His eyes looked at me in confusion.

I admitted that he had never played a major role in my life. He had never given me a safe place to fall. I couldn't run to him when I got scared. I had to figure my life out without his guidance.

I thanked him honestly, and said that, because of our ambiguous relationship, I became a strong-willed, intelligent and independent woman.

One thing that my dad definitely gifted me with was a very dry sense of humour. In honour of that, I pushed the envelope one step further in my conversation with him that afternoon.

Being the youngest of three girls, I said to him, "And furthermore, Dad, I know I was your last chance at having a son. But God sent you an Angel, instead!" He smiled.

I strongly felt my Grandmother in spirit in his room, and told him that his Mom was waiting to take him home. He smiled and weakly nodded.

I reminded him that I am a Psychic Medium, and teasingly told him that he better "check in" with me when he made it to the Other Side. Again, he nodded.

Then I gave him a kiss on his forehead, and I left the nursing home, not knowing for certain that it would be our final exchange. In spite of my dominating that conversation, I could almost feel my Dad replying to my words.

He died very early the next morning.

This was an amazing experience for me, and such a beautiful final gift that we gave to each other. Not only was I able to forgive him, and accept our relationship as an absolute blessing, but I also had the chance to thank him before he died. We cleared our slate.

It took Dad almost two years after that to make direct contact with me from the Other Side. I was performing Platform Mediumship for a class, and all of a sudden I heard his voice beneath my ear. He called me by a childhood nickname that I had totally forgotten about!

I stopped in my tracks, excused myself to the class, and had a brief but moving conversation with him. It was over in minutes, but the memory of that lives on in my heart. Dad made good on his word!

I have been told, by the Wise Ones on the Other Side, that those who hurt us or disappointed us the most in this life are the ones who love us the most on the Other Side.

For whatever reason, they contracted the role they played in our lifetime in order to teach us the toughest life lessons.

When you trust in that awareness, you can begin to forgive those who caused you harm and pain. In doing so, the healing begins and you can move forward with a much lighter heart.

"Peace begins when expectations end".
(Sri Chinmoy)

ALOHA!

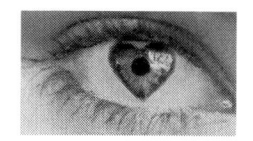

The Hawaiian word "Aloha" means both hello and farewell. In its truest context, the word means love, peace and compassion. I bid you all of the above.

If you made it to this chapter, allow me to express to you my sincere appreciation and gratitude for taking the time to read this book.

Writing <u>If You Could See the World Through My Eyes</u> has been my labour of love from start to finish, and everywhere in between!

Recounting some of these stories has been both cathartic and healing for me at the same time. Thank you. Perhaps you will also find some healing in the stories that have been told.

Were it not for those who believed in me, both in the physical and in Spirit, this couldn't have come together so swiftly. At times, my fingers were literally flying on the keyboard, which is usually an indicator that my friends in Spirit were helping me to write. I am so blessed.

When we are Divinely inspired to do something, and when we get out of our own way, everything seems to flow. So many times I'd be pecking away at the keyboard, and discover that hours and hours had passed without my even being aware of it! Time truly does fly when you're having fun.

Oftentimes in composing this book, my Guides would tell me to avoid "perfectionism", (perfectionism doesn't really exist on this planet anyhow!). They felt it was more important to focus on getting the messages out instead.

Please forgive me if I've left a few particles dangling, or have incorrectly punctuated some sentences. I'm only human, after all!

A few years ago, I was "instant messaging" with a friend. We were conversing back and forth, having fun, and finally he said, "Stop writing the way you talk! I can literally hear your voice when I'm reading your messages!"

If you feel that you could hear my voice while reading this book, you're probably correct. I write straight from my heart.

The life lessons continue, and the stories will accumulate. I could write forever, but at some point you have to hit the "gong" and wrap things up.

I felt it was important to talk about some (but not all) ways of being in this life, and some (but not all) of the lessons I've learned along the way. It has been wonderful sharing with you. I know that there will be more to share in due time.

Be **GRATEFUL** for all you have, and for all that is coming your way. You are much richer than you think! Count your blessings and appreciate that your cup overflows.

Be **OPEN-MINDED** and strive to learn something new every day. The world is rich with opportunities to expand your knowledge. Seek them out.

Be **DISCERNING**, and don't get taken for a ride. Trust your gut instincts. They won't fail you.

Be **PRESENT** and don't miss out on a single precious moment in life. You can never reclaim lost time.

Be **POSITIVE** and things in life won't seem as difficult. Change your perception and look for the silver linings. They are there.

Be **ACCEPTING** and understand that you don't have the ability or right to control anyone's life but your own.

Be **WILLING TO BREAK A SWEAT!** Life isn't a dress rehearsal! Take ownership of your life, dive right in, and fulfill your wildest dreams.

Be **KIND** to others, and be even kinder to yourself. In the grand scheme of things, you matter most.

Be **FORGIVING** of those who wronged you. Forgive yourself if you have wronged others. Ask to be sent opportunities to do better next time, and then DO better next time.

Your story isn't over yet, and neither is mine. I hope that the stories and lessons contained in this book will assist you in living your life in a more meaningful manner.

Until we meet again, I will continue to send you my love and I will pray for your peace and happiness.

Much love,
Andrea Claire

For more information about
Psychic Medium Andrea Claire
please visit www.andreaclaire.ca

If you're interested in booking a session
(either in person or by phone)
please call/text 905.704.9006
or send an email to andreaclaire@cogeco.ca
and we will make it happen!

It would be my honour to be of service.

Made in the USA
Columbia, SC
16 July 2017